LOVE FLOWED DOWN

...IT WAS FOR ME!

Ruth Christian

PRESS

Acknowledgements

I give the sincerest thanks to a very precious group of people, who made the writing and completion of this book possible: to Kristy Rinner, for her countless hours spent editing the manuscript and her desire to help me create one that is well-written; to Teresa Muller, who inspired me to write the book and read the manuscript for content, giving input and encouragement throughout the writing process; to Pastors Dwight Douville, Steve Shepard and Danny Bond, who supported me in this endeavor; to so many brothers and sisters in Christ, who have prayed this book to completion and encouraged me continually; to Dana Smith, who in the very beginning read the first few chapters and encouraged me to continue on; to Mom, who continues to love her daughter and has given financial support; to Jim Rinner for his help in preparing a photograph for the back cover; to Xulon Press for their desire to help Christian writers such as myself get their books published; and last, but not least, to my Lord and Savior, Jesus Christ, whose love changed my life and is the true inspiration for the writing of this book.

Table of Contents

Journal:

March 10, 1990: "Father, I pray that you would help me write about homosexuality, my life and pick out Scriptures that relate and are appropriate. I think I could help others."

August 25, 1990: *"Lord, Pastor Dwight feels You might have working with gays in store for me. I would love to do Your will in that area. I pray that might be part of Your plan for me. Father, help me to write up some thoughts that could help me and help others counsel in this area. Help me to pull all the right Scriptures together…"*

Scriptures:

1 John 5:14-15 "Now this is the confidence that we have in Him, that if we ask anything according to His will, He hears us. And if we know that He hears us, whatever we ask, we know that we have the petitions that we have asked of Him."

Psalm 37: 5, 7a "Commit your way to the LORD, trust also in Him, and He shall bring it to pass… Rest in the LORD, and wait patiently for Him."

James 4:10 "Humble yourselves in the sight of the Lord, and He will lift you up."

In God's time He answered, "Yes" to this prayer of mine that I repeatedly recorded in my journal as a young believer. It would take 15 years of preparation before *Bridge of Hope Ministry* was born!

Journal excerpts were edited for grammar, punctuation and clarity. Identifying personal information may have been omitted. Names may have been changed.

Introduction

It all started when I began to feel restlessness in my spirit. I already had a wonderful life, full with purpose and meaning as I walked with Jesus and lived-out His will for my life. Just four years before, God had called me to leave my 28-year teaching career. I had been praying about retiring early so I could go into fulltime Christian work, but it had to be God's will for my life. By His Spirit and the Word of God, the Lord spoke to me three times in a few days through Hebrews 11:8: "Abraham went out, not knowing where he was going." So, taking a giant step of faith, I put in for a year's leave from teaching with no intention of returning, "not knowing where I was going." In three months, God opened the door for me to work in my church office. I was already teaching women's Bible studies and overseeing the Women's Ministry. After some adjustments, I settled into this new season of fulltime Christian work, so blessed and *comfortable*. Now why did I have this restlessness within? Initially, I thought perhaps the Lord was going to open doors of opportunity to teach women outside of my church or to counsel women on a larger scale at my church.

Then I got a phone call from a friend who was going to minister to a few young adults. Two of the young men had been living the homosexual lifestyle and had recently accepted Jesus as their Savior. Knowing the topic of homosexuality and issues related to it would surely enter into their discussions, she asked how I would minister to them. My immediate thought was, "You've been walking with the Lord over 30 years, and you're asking me!" But, you see, when I was born again, I had come out of a 15-year lesbian lifestyle. I began sharing some thoughts when she interrupted, and said, "You should have a website... ministry in this area is so needed!" I remember thinking, "I don't really want a new ministry! I like what I'm doing, thank you very much!" I would occasionally hand out audio recordings of my testimony and talk with people who had questions because someone they knew was gay. "That's enough, God!" was my thinking. Well, to make a long story short, God *was* calling me to new ministry. After four days with little sleep and much prayer, as well as a time of wrestling with God, He confirmed the call in my heart. *Bridge of Hope Ministry* was born; its purpose is to minister to those people struggling with same-sex attractions and to those people seeking to come out of homosexuality. But, the ministry is also to help my brothers and sisters in Christ minister to those people who they know and love and are gay.

Along with the call to this new ministry, God lit a fire deep within me to minister the love of Jesus! Here's what I wrote in my journal, April 22, 2005: *"Lord, in the past few days, You have given me a vision for the new ministry, so, Lord, as I plan, I know You will direct my steps (Proverbs 16:9). Lord, Your will be done. This is your ministry… and like Mary, I am your servant. '"Behold the maidservant of the Lord! Let it be to me according to Your Word"' (Luke 1:38). '"Blessed is she who believed, for there will be a fulfillment of those things which were told her from the Lord"' (Luke 1:45). And Lord, just like those on the road to Emmaus (Luke 24:32), You spoke and kindled this fire within!"*

So, what is Bridge of Hope Ministry? It is a three-fold ministry. First, it is a website through which I can advise and encourage by my testimony, Bible studies, journal excerpts, messages and email. Second, it is the book you hold in your hands. Third, it is my availability to speak at churches, Christian schools and Christian organizations to share my testimony and to minister to young and old.

My prayer is that everyone who reads this book understands that it is a testimony of the love of God that truly changes lives. His love is manifested through His awesome grace and mercy to everyone who trusts in Him! And, this love comes through a person: Jesus Christ! In the following pages, you will find my testimony as well as the things I've learned along the way that were foundational for true change to take place in my life. And through the process of writing this book, I have a wonderful opportunity like the writer of Psalm 77 to "meditate on all Your work, and talk of Your deeds" (v. 1). As you read what I write about what God has done in my life, please understand my heart: "I will praise You, O LORD, with my whole heart; I will tell of all Your marvelous works" (Psalm 9:1). Amen!

Let's begin...

Journal:

January 7, 1990: *"I've been a Christian now for almost a year and five months, and so much has happened. Lord, You've really been working in me, and I wish I had it all documented. Lord, I praise You and thank You so much for saving me. Your grace is truly a blessing. Lord, I pray I can be a loving and forgiving Christian. Lord, I pray for you to continue to mold me and shape me into the person you want me to be. I want you in control of my life. I desire to do Your will, Father."*

Scriptures:

Psalm 30: 2-3, 12 "O Lord my God, I cried out to You, and You healed me. O Lord, You brought my soul up from the grave; You have kept me alive, that I should not go down to the pit… To the end that my glory [soul] may sing praise to You and not be silent. O Lord my God, I will give thanks to You forever."

John 3: 6-8 "That which is born of the flesh is flesh, and that which is born of the Spirit is spirit. Do not marvel that I said to you, "You must be born again." The wind blows where it wishes, and you hear the sound of it, but cannot tell where it comes from and where it goes. So is everyone who is born of the Spirit.'"

Chapter 1: The Miracle of a New Creation

L et me begin by asking you a very important question! Do you believe in miracles? I do! I believe every true salvation testimony is the story of a regenerated heart, where God has done a supernatural work in our innermost being. My testimony that I am about to share with you is a true miracle that declares how God's love, grace and mercy have truly changed my life from the inside out. It's important to understand that what God has done in my life, He can do in anyone's life. Let me ask you this: Has God done a miracle in your life? Do you have a testimony?

Contemporary Christian song writer and recording artist, Stephen Bennett has a wonderful song entitled "Do You Have a Testimony?"[1]

The first verse asks two important questions:

Do you have a testimony, a day you can recall
When you gave your life to Jesus – your heart,
*   your mind, your soul?*
Is there an hour that you know, when you were
*   born again;*
A new creation came forth and the old came to
*   an end?*

My heart reply is, "Oh, yes, I can recall such a day! Thank you, God!" But before I take you to that day, let me give you a thumbnail picture of my life before that day.

I grew up in Des Plaines, Illinois, a northwest suburb of Chicago. My family consisted of my mom, my dad and my brother, who was six and a half years older than me. My dad worked hard as a truck driver for a construction company. My mom was a stay-at-home mom most of the years I was growing up. My parents loved us and impressed on my brother and me the importance of family.

I had a happy childhood living out in the country where we all had big yards and some open fields to play in. I was free to roam around the neighborhood and not fear for my safety. In the neighborhood, there were more boys my age than girls, so most of my friends were boys. Because I was a tomboy and had good athletic ability, I enjoyed playing baseball, basketball and football with my friends. We rode our bikes everywhere. It did not matter what season of the year we were in, we tried to play outside. In the winter we built snow forts, went sledding and ice-skated on our neighborhood creek. When we could not be outside, we met at someone's house and often played board games, ping-pong, darts, make believe games, etc. We even acted out TV detective shows or various westerns. I usually played the part of one of the male characters. One summer, we studied the Plains Indians and their dances and put on a show for the neighborhood. We made costumes and charged a nickel admission. Throughout my elementary school days, we often got together to play before it was time to be home for supper. And, concerning school, I enjoyed learning and challenged myself to get good grades. Overall, I really have good memories of my childhood.

Just before I entered junior high, our family was forced to move into town, where my parents bought a smaller home, with a small yard on a busy road. This was a stressful time for the family. My tomboy days, however, were over, and by the eighth grade, my new best friend was one of the most popular girls in school. Her popularity remained throughout our high school years. This was quite a change from my childhood days when my closest friends were boys. While I was well-liked during my junior and senior high years, I felt I could never measure up to my "popular" best friend. Our friendship grew to be unhealthy, as she was very controlling, and I became emotionally-dependent on her. One summer, we often went in her basement to play 45 records and dance. This was the beginning of "rock" dancing... you know, no longer hanging on to your partner when you fast danced.

Well, one day, we put on a slow song and danced, with me taking on the boy's part, which I thought nothing of. But, same-sex attractions and feelings appeared, and because we were at an age where our hormones had kicked in, it wasn't long before we acted upon the feelings and kissed. That began a physical relationship. When it first happened, I remember thinking, "We are just acting like when we used to act out the TV shows and westerns." During this period of time, I was still attracted to boys, so I dated and had boyfriends throughout high school. While I never thought about permanently living this lifestyle that had developed with my girlfriend, at times she definitely came before anyone else, male or female. During junior and senior high school I never had same-sex attractions for anyone else. We went to different colleges, and that separation freed me from my emotional dependency on her and the same-sex attractions went away. She met a young man in college and got married; she never lived the homosexual lifestyle. However, I took a different path.

Now, before I go any further and talk about the path I took, I must mention one other major influence on my development as a child and as a person. My parents tried to raise us according to Judeo-Christian values. While they themselves did not attend church very often, they made sure we went to Sunday school. From my early childhood through my high school years, I attended several different Protestant-denomination churches. In high school, I was even involved in the youth group. I believed in God, but

I had not heard about having a personal relationship with Him.

I attended college from 1967-71, receiving a bachelor's degree in education with a broad-field major in physical education. I participated in and excelled in sports throughout my college years, which eventually lead to my induction into the University of Wisconsin-Whitewater Athletic Hall of Fame. While sports were an important part of my life, I also found myself on a search for spiritual truth. I would occasionally attend the Catholic, folk-guitar masses on campus. While I sensed certain things about those guitar masses were what God intended for a gathering of believers, I still did not find the spiritual truth for questions that needed to be answered: Why were there so many different denominations in Christianity? What was it that was supposed to make us true Christians? That we had the same traditions when it came to Christmas and Easter? What about heaven? Where did it fit in all of this? I do not remember sin ever being discussed or hearing that Jesus had died for my sin and thereby made a way for me to have a relationship with God. I did not understand sin was the issue and that Jesus bridged the gap between sinful man and a Holy God! When I graduated and got my first teaching job, I stopped going to church and searching for spiritual truth.

Now, at this point, as you think about my college days, a very important question must come to mind. Where did boys fit into my life? Well, just like in my early teen years, late teen and early adult years, I was still attracted to boys. My high school girlfriend and that relationship were now out of the picture. The very first week of college, I met a young man, and we began to date. Those were complicated days, both in our nation and in my personal life. I really felt I loved him and vice versa. We were close to becoming engaged. I believe his main motivation for attending college was to keep from being drafted. At the end of the first semester of our sophomore year, due to poor grades and a lack of interest in college, he decided to enlist. This meant that after basic training he would surely go to Viet Nam. Before he left for his army physical and basic training, we had a very difficult and emotional, yet wonderful evening together. But just two days later, he surprised me by calling from the lobby of my college dormitory. He was back for good; he had flunked his physical! I was so relieved he was not going to Viet Nam and excited that he was back!

But how quickly things changed, and in a few months, something happened. Same-sex attractions and feelings surfaced for the second time in my life. This time it was for a woman who was my teammate on our basketball team. Our relationship crossed the line from emotional to physical as we acted upon these feelings. At this point, I lead a double life until I broke up with the young man after almost three years together. But even with this second wrong relationship, it was not my desire to lead only this lifestyle. And you must remember, during the late 60s and early 70s, almost everyone living the homosexual lifestyle was living it "in the closet."

After I graduated from college, during my first two years of teaching, I dated a few of the single guys who taught at the school. We had a great, young staff that enjoyed spending time together after school events on Friday and Saturday nights. During the summer, I decided to play on a women's softball team. I became good friends with a woman on the team. At that time, same-sex attractions surfaced and lead to a three-year relationship with that woman. It was then that I chose to lead the homosexual life-style. We lived in Fort Lauderdale, Florida for two years, where for the first time, I went to gay bars and acquired a network of gay friends. While living in Florida, I had a very serious work-related accident. I believe God was trying to get my attention in many ways. I certainly knew I was "lucky" to be alive, and I thanked God. A year after I recuperated from the accident, I moved up to Menasha, Wisconsin to take a teaching position that I held for 28 years.

So, I lead a lesbian lifestyle for about 15 years, but there were the previous 10 years where I had same-sex attraction feelings that I acted upon. I lived in secret all those years, not wanting people to know the "real" me. Initially, in the mid 70s, deep down inside, I believed this lifestyle was wrong. It was at that time that psychologists and psychiatrists determined that homosexuality was not a mental and/or emotional disorder, but that homosexuals were born that way. It did not take long for me to buy into that lie. My thinking was this: "I'm a good person, and I was just created to love in this manner. I did not ask to have these attractions and feelings for women. They were just there! How could this be wrong?" It was easy to convince myself that I was born that way. Through the years, I occasionally went to church and a few times even heard a sermon that said homosexuality was wrong. Nevertheless, by the next day I would block it out of my mind and keep living according to my fleshly feelings, desires and thinking.

The homosexual/lesbian lifestyle is profoundly self-serving and self-indulgent. While I felt I was very committed to my partner, my relationships only lasted two-to-five years. Emotional dependency on another person is usually at the core of lesbian relationships, as it was in my relationships. Alcohol was a huge part of the lifestyle I was entrenched in, both with my partners and with my network of gay friends. Finally, in 1986, I was deeply hurt when the person I was with left me for a relationship with a man, and, in just a year, married him. I had always been the one to break up the relationship; I certainly never had someone leave me to marry a man. I was "blown away", and it started me on a downward spiral into the pit. There is a song we have sung many times in church called "What Wondrous Love" that always reminds me of my situation right before the love of God rescued me. How I can relate to these verses:

> *What wondrous love is this*
> *That caused the Lord of bliss*
> *To bear the dreadful curse*
> *For my soul, for my soul*
> *To bear the dreadful curse for my soul*

*When I was sinking down, sinking down, sinking
down*
When I was sinking down, sinking down

When I was sinking down
Beneath God's righteous frown
Christ laid aside His crown
For my soul, for my soul
Christ laid aside His crown for my soul [2]

By the summer of 1988, I was almost in the pit
of despair. As the saying goes, I didn't know if I was
"on foot or horse-back." I could not find relationships
that made me happy, that met my needs. I almost had
an affair with a man while I was having a physical
relationship with a woman who I really did not like
very much. I had a huge void deep inside that needed
to be filled! I was back living the double life, and I
had absolutely no peace in my life. My life was a
mess! But, this turned out to be a very good thing.
God finally had me in a place where He could work
in my life.

In August of that summer, I worked a professional
golf tournament. It was my job to oversee the food
service in a corporate hospitality tent. The vice-pres-
ident of the corporation brought his daughter, Jill, to
be the hostess for that week. She was a replacement
for the corporate hostess who could not be there,
but she was God's choice for hostess all along. We
immediately started to develop a friendship, as she
spent more time with the "help" than she did with
the business and corporate people who would come

into the tent. At the conclusion of the final day of the tournament, a group of us decided to go out for pizza. I rode with Jill, and by the providence of God, we lost everyone else when we left the country club. God had a plan. She took me to my hometown where I was staying with my parents, and we went to my old high school hangout for pizza. I knew she would soon be starting a new job. She had just graduated from college, so I thought the job was the beginning of her career in finance. During our conversation I found out the job was only temporary as she was raising support to go into full-time Christian work. I actually found it all very interesting. It also came up during our discussion that she had never spent time in Wisconsin. When she dropped me off at my parents' home, I invited her to come up sometime. And in just two weeks, she came up for a weekend visit.

Saturday morning as we sipped our coffee and talked, religion and spiritual "stuff" came up. One of the things I told her was that I believed in God and that it bothered me that I was never confirmed. As we talked, I felt lead to tell Jill the lifestyle I was leading and what had gone on the past two years. She said something like this: "Ruth, I believe it (homosexuality) is wrong because the Bible says it is. God loves you and so do I, but that is something you need to take to God." She left it at that, never mentioning it again. On Sunday while we were out for lunch, she brought out "The Four Spiritual Laws" tract published by Campus Crusade for Christ. [3] She opened up to the page where there are two circles: one with self in the center and the other with Christ in the center. Each circle represents a person's life. Jill asked, "Ruth, which circle best represents your life? Who is on the throne of your life? Who is in control?"

I responded, "A little bit of both," meaning a little bit of God and a little bit of self, probably because I believed in God and had occasionally prayed. Yet the truth was, self was very much in control of my life. After my response, Jill asked, "Which circle would you like to be representative of your life?" I replied, "The one with Christ in the center." For about an hour, we had a discussion concerning some of the truths in the tract. I don't remember any of the other specifics of our conversation. At the end of our discussion, Jill asked if I wanted to pray to receive Jesus into my life. I was really meditating on all we had discussed, but I was not ready to make that decision. She had to travel home that evening, so she gave me the tract and both of us were left with "things" to ponder. One of the things I pondered was this wonderful new friendship with Jill that was developing. Jill was pondering my seriousness in thinking things through during our discussion, when the Lord spoke to her heart that I was going to receive Him very soon.

The next morning, Monday, August 22, 1988, I sat down in my favorite chair with a cup of coffee and read through "The Four Spiritual Laws," cover to cover. It said I could receive Christ right then by faith through prayer. I prayed the suggested prayer and meant it with all my heart!

"Lord Jesus, I need You. Thank You for dying on the cross for my sins. I open the door of my life and receive You as my Savior and Lord. Thank You for forgiving my sins and giving me eternal life. Take control of the throne of my life. Make me the kind of person You want me to be." [4]

This was the truth I had been searching for. Immediately, it was as if this tremendous weight was lifted off my shoulders. I began to cry like a baby, with tears of joy. I received such an incredible inner-peace that I had never experienced before. For the first time in my life, I knew God was not only real, but also personal, and that I could have a relationship with Him. It was a beautiful summer day, and I walked outside with wet eyes, and my neighbor happened to be standing in the driveway; "Ruth, what is wrong?" she asked. I told her I had just prayed to accept Jesus into my life. She started to cry and said she had prayed for me. You see, several years before, I had lived in this duplex with a woman, and Marilyn had lived on the other side. Recently, I had moved back... another circumstance God had set up. She invited me to go to her church on Sunday. The tract said to find a Bible-teaching church. The Lord already had one lined-up for me, and Marilyn's church became my home-church the very first Sunday after I was saved.

Now, there was one more important thing I did that day that jump-started my walk with the Lord. The tract suggested that you start reading the Bible, starting at the Gospel of John. So, as soon as I came back inside, I grabbed and opened my rarely-used Bible that was sitting in a prominent position on my entertainment center. I found the Gospel of John and read the whole book that day. Because of the Holy Spirit inside, my eyes were open with understanding now. This was the beginning of my thirst for the Word of God. I remember reading John 3:7, where Jesus tells Nicodemus he must be born again. I remember thinking, "Wow, that's what just happened to me!" I had no doubt. I called Jill later that day to tell her what happened. She was so excited and immediately began to disciple me through letters, phone conversations and visits. God used our relationship to show me what a healthy friendship with a woman should be like, and I would soon begin to deal with emotional dependency issues.

As a new believer, I was so thankful to attend a church that taught the Word of God. I spent as much time reading and studying the Bible as I could. I listened to Christian radio and watched Christian TV. I began reading good Christian books that gave the Biblical perspective on different aspects of Christian living. I always got input from mature Christians concerning the books I read. The truth and application in those books was based on the Word of God, not man's wisdom. I began to grow in my faith, immediately!

So, I do have a glorious day I can recall where I gave my heart, my mind, and my soul to Jesus and became a new creature in Him! I accepted Jesus as my Savior and my Lord. From the very beginning, it was my desire that He be the Lord of my life. My life had been a mess with me in control; I needed Him to take control of the throne of my life. For me, a person coming out of the homosexual lifestyle, this would be very important for complete change to take place... to be completely heterosexual in my thoughts, feelings and identity. It's important for you to understand, I accepted the Lord knowing I was a sinner, but not really thinking about the lifestyle I had been leading. I remember thinking, "Now what? Could I be truly heterosexual?" I would still have same-sex attraction feelings to deal with for a period of time. Would these go away?

There is another verse from Stephen Bennett's song I want to share...

> *Do you have a testimony that the world can plainly see,*
> *That from the life you used to live, you have truly been set free?*
> *Are you sold out for Jesus, and His Name you now proclaim?*
> *Now that you've become a Christian, it seems everything has changed.*[5]

This verse truly describes my life since that day I gave my heart, my mind and my soul to Jesus. Being born again of the Spirit is as much a miracle of God as is our physical birth. Yes, I truly was set free. Everything changed! Make no mistake about it, this is about being able to come out of the homosexual lifestyle and be healed of the same-sex attractions and feelings. It's about becoming a person with true heterosexual desires, attractions and feelings as well as becoming the person God created me to be. Does it mean that on the day I was born again, all the same-sex attractions, feelings and desires disappeared immediately? No, but they did in time! They never became a roadblock in my walk with the Lord. I immediately got into reading and studying God's Word where the promises of God gave me such hope. One of those promises became my life verse. Romans 8:1 says: "There is therefore now no condemnation for those who are in Christ Jesus." This verse so ministered to me, and kept me from looking back, from being burdened with my past sins. Actually, there is condemnation that goes with the homosexual lifestyle, both real and perceived, but I had such a peace and joy inside knowing I wasn't that person anymore. Oh, thank you, Jesus!

You might be thinking, "What did you do to be set free from bondage to the homosexual lifestyle? How were you set free? What did you do that everything changed in time?" Well, I'm glad you asked these questions. I will answer them in the pages ahead! We will look at the reality of Ruth becoming a new creation in Christ Jesus (2 Corinthians 5:17). The first step for me was to acknowledge and to agree with the truth of God's Word that says homosexuality is sin. So, let's take some time to look at the sin issue next!

"I faced this question about the biblical perspective on homosexuality. As an eighteen-year-old college freshman, I discovered an impressive array of books on homosexuality at the university library... As I read page after page of arguments justifying same-sex practices, my mind wanted so much to believe the words I was reading. **I f only I could really embrace this viewpoint,** *I thought,* **all of the conflict I feel inside would be resolved.**

"But, as hard as I tried to block it out, a stronger conviction refused to budge from my conscience: **This book is wrong. These arguments are wrong. Homosexuality is wrong!**

"Tears of frustration came to my eyes as I realized that, no matter how much time I spent reading why homosexuality was an acceptable option for the Christian, I would never be able to believe it. I knew too much about the Biblical stand on sex outside of marriage. Whether sex occurred between an unmarried man and woman or between two same-sex partners, the activity would always be fornication or adultery. No amount of justification or argument would change God's standard.

"So I had a clear choice to make: Would I obey God's Word, or seek to reinterpret it in order to fulfill my sexual desires?" [1]

Chapter 2: Sin Is the Issue

As I shared in the previous chapter, I believed in God from an early age and considered myself a Christian. If someone had asked me if I thought I would go to heaven, I would have replied, "Yes!" Why? Because I thought I was a good person. But, I could never be good enough because God requires perfection. I did not understand that from God's perspective, sin was a huge issue in my life. Although I believed in God, in reality, my sin separated me from Him. Before I was born again, I never considered myself a sinner, nor did I really understand what sin is. Oh, in magazines, I saw these weird hippies being baptized, and in various places I read statements like: "Jesus saves;" "Repent sinner; you must be born again;" "John 3:16." I thought these "Jesus freaks" were all wacko, just like I thought those people in the drug culture of the day who were living in San Francisco were all wacko. I did not understand that many of the "Jesus freaks" had actually come out of the drug culture and had been truly changed. I lumped them all into the same category. After all, I had gone to all these established Christian-denominational churches and had not heard this "weird stuff."

Now, it occurs to me that perhaps you are reading this, and you are new to the Bible or to this "born again stuff." Do you understand that from God's perspective, sin is the issue for all of mankind? And, quite likely, there are others of you who are about ready to slam the book shut and quit reading any further because the word "sin" conjures up feelings of hatred. Why? Well, because of the unloving way you have had the "sin issue" pushed at you from some people in the church. That is not my intent at all. Simply put, it's my intent and desire to speak God's truth in love, just like my friend Jill spoke it to me. The truth is this: what the Bible calls sin separates us from God now and for all of eternity if we do not deal with it His way. So, what is sin, anyway?

Sin means "to miss the mark and therefore not win the prize." It's like an arrow missing the target during a competition, except when we sin, we miss the mark of God's standard of righteousness. We cannot receive the "prize of righteousness," the prize of being in right-standing with God. According to the Bible, sin is disobedience to God. That's what happened in the very beginning, in the Garden of Eden when Adam and Eve ate from the tree of the knowledge of good and evil. The very first man and woman disobeyed God (Genesis 1-3). The following Scriptures give us further insight into sin: To know the right thing to do and not to do it is sin (James

4:17). Whatever is not of faith is sin (Romans 14:23) because faith is choosing to take God at His word. Therefore, unbelief is sin because it leads to disobedience. Sin is lawlessness (1 John 3:4). And finally, sin is man's going astray and turning to his own way (Isaiah 53:6). I think this is enough to give us the big picture of sin; you get the idea.

Let's be honest! The truth is we all have disobeyed God somewhere along the line. We all have done our own thing in some manner or another. In other words, we have turned from God's way of living life to our own way of living life. I find it interesting that in the late 60s and the early 70s, I honestly thought I was on the straight and narrow path because I wasn't tripping-out on drugs and dropping out of society, or participating in social protests, or getting into the free-love mentality. No, I could be found loving my family and my friends, going to church and getting an education so I would have a noble career as a teacher. And during a time when purity was out and having sex with your boyfriend was in, I refused to go that far. Now, it's not that loving others, going to church and getting an education were bad, but from God's perspective, I was in the same camp as the drug users or those participating in free-love. It was, among other things, my self-righteousness that put me there. Then throw in the reality that I was acting upon the same-sex attractions and feelings that surfaced, and eventually, I decided to live the lesbian lifestyle. The point I'm trying to make here is that from God's perspective, I, too, had gone astray and turned to my own way. I, indeed, was a sinner like everyone else.

So, how are we to deal with the sin in our life? The wonderful reality is that Jesus did what needed to be done. He paid the penalty for our sin, for my sin and for yours, when He died on the cross; He paid a huge debt that we could never pay. The question is why did He do that? God created man to have fellowship with Him, meaning an intimate loving relationship, and that fellowship was broken in the garden when man sinned. But praise God; He loved us so much He had a plan to redeem us! "For God so loved the world that He gave His only begotten Son, that who ever believes in Him should not perish but have everlasting life" (John 3:16). Because "all have sinned and fallen short of the glory of God" (Romans 3:23), we cannot fellowship with a holy God. But in Christ, God has reconciled the world to Himself (2 Corinthians 5:19). Our part is to believe and receive Him, then we become children of God (John 1:12). Oh what love, that God "made [Jesus] who knew no sin to be sin for us, that we might become the righteousness of God in Him" (2 Corinthians 5:21). All of my sin and all of your sin was put upon Jesus, and in return, we receive His righteousness. That's a fantastic deal; the great exchange takes place when, by faith, we receive Jesus as our Savior and Lord; then the Holy Spirit comes and takes up residence inside of us. We have a new heart... a regenerate heart. Therefore we become new creatures in Christ (2 Corinthians 5:17). The Holy Spirit of God can accomplish a life-changing transformation in everyone who will only believe in Christ and allow Him to be the Lord of their lives. This surrender is

essential if a person is going to come out of homosexuality and be truly changed. This surrendering,
however, is where some fall short. They do not want
to give up control of their life! Why?

I believe there are two main reasons those who are
born again may not want to come out of the homosexual lifestyle. First of all, they have a homosexual
identity and same-sex attractions, feelings and desires
that they have developed, which do not immediately
go away when they are born again. Why and how
they developed in the first place, I will cover later in
the book. But when they are not immediately healed
of these things, they want to cash it in: "This born
again thing must not have worked; I am not attracted
to the opposite sex. And I love my partner and my
life; I want Jesus because I know I'm a sinner, but this
is just who I am! It's just another way to love; I've
known I was gay since I was five years old." They
walk by feelings and the lusts of the flesh and not by
faith. They continue to be deceived into thinking, "I
had to have been born this way." They do not understand these things took time to develop, and it will
take time for them to be replaced with proper attractions, feelings, thinking and identity. For almost three
years after I was born again, I had same-sex attractions and feelings that would surface from time to
time. I also had emotional dependency issues to work
through. But in His time, God healed me of all these
things. What He did for me, He can do for anyone
who desires to come out of the homosexual lifestyle
and be completely changed! And please understand,
the change I'm talking about here is to be completely

heterosexual: to be the man or woman God created you to be, with feelings and desires for the opposite sex, and to be a man or woman with a heterosexual identity with an appreciation for manhood, if you are a man, or womanhood, if you are a woman!

The second reason a person may not be successful in coming out of the homosexual lifestyle is that they will not accept by faith what the Bible says about homosexuality. It is sin! They may agree with God that they are a sinner and needed Jesus, but they continue to be deceived and will not agree with God that homosexuality is wrong. How could homosexuality be wrong? They only know that they did not ask for these attractions and feelings for the same-sex, and so they walk by feelings and not by faith in God and in His Word. After I was born again, I soon learned that specific Scriptures say homosexuality is sin, but they also gave me hope that I could change. Let's look at just two portions of God's Word that talk about homosexuality.

The first place we want to look is in Romans 1:26-27:

> "For this reason God gave them up to vile passions. For even their women exchanged the natural use for what is against nature. Likewise also the men, leaving the natural use of the woman, burned in their lust for one another, men with men committing what is shameful, and receiving in themselves the penalty of their error which was due."

It is clear in these verses that having physical relations with a person of your same sex is sin, for both males and females. It is in the list of things the unrighteous do (vv. 29-31), and furthermore, verse 32 declares that those who practice such things continually are deserving of death (that is, spiritual separation from God). So, the idea in the verses is you keep on practicing homosexuality, you keep living the lifestyle, and if you do that, then you will experience spiritual separation from God.

The second truth about homosexuality we want to look at is 1 Corinthians 6:9-11:

> "Do you not know that the unrighteous will not inherit the kingdom of God? Do not be deceived. Neither fornicators, nor idolaters, nor adulterers, nor homosexuals, nor sodomites, nor thieves, nor covetous, nor drunkards, nor revilers, nor extortioners will inherit the kingdom of God. And **such were** some of you. But you were washed, but you were sanctified, but you were justified in the name of the Lord Jesus and by the Spirit of our God." (Emphasis mine!)

The context of these verses is Paul telling the Corinthian church to deal with immorality in the church (read 1Corinthians 5:9-11). He commands them not to be deceived! Those living the lifestyles mentioned here, which includes homosexuality and sodomy, are unrighteous, but it does not have to be that way. For a believer coming out of homosexuality, verse 11 is a wonderful truth. *"And **such were some of you.**"* (Emphasis mine, again!) Paul knew that some people in the church had been homosexuals, but no longer were. Oh, I remember when I first read this truth in the Bible; I could not believe it. "Wow, the Bible says I can change!" The homosexual can change and become truly heterosexual from the inside out!

It is clear the Bible says homosexuality is sin. It is only when a person takes Scriptures out of context and twists them to say what they want them to say that the truth is not clear. The question is, do you want to change? If you are born again, let me ask you several questions that you can answer in your own heart. Do you want to please God? Or better yet, do you love Jesus? Jesus says if we love Him we will keep His commandments (John 14:15). Do you love Jesus more than your homosexuality? Do you have a regenerate heart or not? In other words, has the Holy Spirit taken up residence inside you, making you a new creation in Christ? Do you even want Him to take control of your life?

Let's look at all of this from one more angle. Let me remind you of a Scripture that describes us before we were born again, while we were in our unregenerate condition. The Bible tells us in Titus 3:3 that we were foolish, disobedient, deceived, serving various lusts and pleasures, living in malice and envy, hateful and hating one another. Now you may be inclined to argue with this assessment. "Oh, no, Ruth, I wasn't all that bad before I become a Christian. I graduated with honors. I was really respected by my peers and loved by my friends. I even gave to those in need." Well, I would have echoed similar sentiments before I was born again, but in reality, that's who I was. Now, however, I am not that same person. I am a new creation in Christ Jesus. What about you?

If you have asked Jesus to come into your life, it means you are agreeing with God that you are a sinner and that homosexuality is sin. If you have no desire to leave the lifestyle, then this verse in Titus describes your current state. You are foolish, disobedient, deceived and serving various lusts and pleasures. Even the apostle Paul, though educated, respected and the holder of an incredible pedigree as a Jew, counted all these things but loss for Christ and rubbish in comparison to the righteousness he gained in Christ. This righteousness can only come if we surrender our lives completely to Christ.

Fortunately, God in His grace and mercy has determined that we do not need to be remembered for our foolishness, disobedience, etc., but we can be remembered for our **faith** in the One who makes fools wise. Paul states in his letter to the Corinthians, "God has chosen the foolish things of the world to put to shame the wise… that no flesh should glory in His presence" (1 Corinthians 1:27-29).

So, if you are a person who is born again and desires to come out of the homosexual lifestyle, you must take a look at who you are from God's point of view, not your own. You must understand His perspective about sin and agree with God that you are a sinner and need a Savior. You must, and this is the harder issue for many people, agree with God that homosexuality is sin and not a proper lifestyle for the child of God. Let me ask you again! Do you love Jesus more than your homosexuality? Then, know this! If you will allow Jesus to be the Lord of your life, then you can be freed from bondage to a sinful lifestyle by the grace He supplies. Surrender, and let God work! God not only saves us by His grace, but by His amazing grace, He also makes us into the man or woman He wants us to be. How, you say? Well, He opens up His storehouse of blessings that cancel the past, equips you for the present and secures your future!

Our part is to believe and to walk in obedience to His Word by the power of the Holy Spirit who dwells in us. That's living faith! If you are a young believer, I understand the same-sex attractions, feelings and desires are probably still there. Hang in there, and walk by faith, not by feelings. Be encouraged by the wonderful promise found in Philippians 1:6: "He who began a good work in you will be faithful to complete it." Do you believe this promise? Without faith, it is impossible to please God (Hebrews 11: 6)! That's why in the next chapter we will try to get a better understanding of living faith!

But before we go there, let me encourage you to do something. If you are not born again, and now you understand the sin issue and that Jesus died for your sin, perhaps you'd like to pray and ask Jesus into your life. Perhaps you say, "I don't know what to pray." Go back to chapter one and pray the prayer I prayed the day I was born again. The important thing is to mean it with all your heart. Then, all of you who are born again, take a moment and give God thanks for saving not only your soul for eternity (heaven awaits!), but also your legacy, reputation and testimony while here on earth. Praise the Lord!

"'Heaven and earth will pass away, but My words shall not pass away'" (Matthew 24:35).

"The word of the Lord abides forever" (1 Peter 1:25).

"The grass withers, the flower fades, but the word of our God stands forever" (Isaiah 40:8).

"These verses were telling me that everything in life may change, but God's Word remains constant. His truth never changes. I was beginning to catch a glimpse of how faith in God's promises could affect me the rest of my life.

"For instance, I feel things very deeply. At times I am so happy I think I will never be sad again. Other times I am so sad I think I will never be happy again... and still other times I feel almost nothing.

"But as strong and as fluctuating as my feelings are, God's Word is

- Truer than anything I feel
- Truer than anything I experience
- Truer than any circumstance I will ever face
- Truer than anything in the world

"Why? Because heaven and earth will pass away, but God's Word will not. This means that no mater how I feel or what I experience, I can choose to depend on the Word of God as the unchanging reality of my life." [1]

Chapter 3: Faith Is Not a Feeling

Very soon after I was born again, I gained a very important Biblical understanding of what faith is and what it is not. Just one month after I was saved, Jill gave me the book <u>Faith Is Not a Feeling</u> by Ney Bailey. This is a classic book, and God knew I needed to hear and to put into practice the message of this book. So, let's get started and take a good look at Biblical faith, and then I'll share with you how a proper understanding of faith was crucial for my coming out of homosexuality!

The Bible tells us in four different places that the "just shall live by faith" (Habakkuk 2:4; Romans 1:17; Galatians 3:11; Hebrews 10:38). When a truth is repeated in God's Word, we can know it is foundational; it is imperative that we have an understanding of that truth. The Bible tells us we are saved by faith and that we are to walk by faith (Ephesians 2:8; 2

Corinthians 5:7); that is, we Christians are to live by faith from the day we are saved. The book of James tells us that real faith is active, not static. It's something we do!

Ok, so what is this faith that we are to live out? We are given a description of faith in Hebrews 11:1: "Now faith is the **substance** of things hoped for, the **evidence** of things not seen" (emphasis mine). True Biblical faith is not a manufactured, "hope-so" kind of feeling, nor is it something we drum-up ourselves. Faith is not faith in faith. Faith is not just an intellectual agreement with a doctrine, nor is it belief without evidence, because that would be superstition. The faith of a believer in Jesus Christ is confident obedience to God's Word in spite of our circumstances or feelings! Let's dig a little deeper into this verse so we can understand biblical faith!

There are two words in verse one that give us further insight into what true faith is; those words are substance and evidence. In the original Greek language of the New Testament, the word translated as "substance" literally means "to stand under; to support". Faith is to a Christian what a foundation is to a house; it is confidence and assurance that he or she will stand. So, you might say, "faith is the confidence of things hoped for". When a believer has faith, it is God's way of giving him or her confidence and assurance that what is promised in the Bible will happen!

The word "evidence" can also be translated "conviction." This is the inward conviction from the indwelling Holy Spirit that convinces us that He will perform what He has promised. For example, in Luke chapter 1 when Mary believes what the angel says, that she would give birth to a baby by the Holy Spirit, it is confirmed by Elizabeth who says concerning Mary: "Blessed is she who believed, for there will be a fulfillment of those things which were told her from the Lord" (Luke 1:45). The same is true for us. Blessed are we when we believe that God will fulfill the promises that He personally speaks to us through His Word. As a result, faith enables us to do what unbelievers cannot do: take God at His Word!

Much of Hebrews chapter 11 is a summary of the lives and the labors of great men and women of faith whose stories are found in the Old Testament. How did they take God at His word? In each case:

1. God spoke to them (His Word)
2. There was that inner conviction that God would do what He promised
3. They obeyed God

Remember, God recognizes this group in the "Hall of Faith" not because they were perfect people, but because they were people of faith! "Without faith it is impossible to please God" (Hebrews 11:6). Faith is the foundation of our lives as Christians. By the grace of God, every child of God is given a measure of faith when we are saved (Romans 12:3). This faith can grow, but please note one very important connection. "Faith comes by hearing, and hearing by the word of God" (Romans 10:17). Being a person of faith is a necessity for all of God's children; it is not just a luxury for a few "super saints."

Faith is not just something we know; faith is something we do. James tells us we are to be doers of His word and not hearers only (James 1:22). Consequently, we practice living, active faith when we are obedient to the Word of God. But here is a very important question: What gets in the way of our obedience to what God is speaking to us? Our feelings and our circumstances get in the way and cause unbelief. Faith is choosing to take God at His Word no matter what our feelings or circumstances are telling us! It's this reality that Ney Bailey brought out so well in her book.

For me and for others coming out of homosexuality, really, for all believers, a Biblical understanding of what faith is and what faith is not is essential for us to walk in a manner worthy of our God. Living-faith operates quite simply. Let's look at it one more time. God speaks through His Word; we trust Him and His Word, and we will ourselves to take Him at His Word, no matter what the circumstances are around us, or what the consequences may be. Our feelings may tell us the circumstances are impossible and the consequences may look frightening, but by real faith, we can obey God and His Word in every situation. In other words, faith is choosing to take God at His Word, not walking by our feelings that are influenced by circumstances and by fiery darts Satan might be shooting at our minds, which cause wrong thinking (Ephesians 6:16; 1 Peter 5:8-9).

Now, let me really take this to a personal level and show you how the proper understanding of faith immediately affected my walk with Jesus. The following are excerpts from my journal (from January and February 1990) when I was only about a year and a half old in the Lord. Please note that in all of my journal excerpts throughout this book, I am always writing to the Lord; I'm sharing my heart with Him.

"Lord, I'm trying to keep my eyes focused on You..."

"I read 1 Corinthians 6 (again), and I had forgotten the impact of verses 9-11 in my life."

"I also know if I wasn't walking with You, I'd probably want this (a relationship with a woman I was coaching with) to be more than a friendship. My faith in You is going to endure. Not all of those old feelings are gone, but faith is not a feeling. Have You created this friendship partly as a test for me? I want to be who You want me to be. I surrender myself to You, Lord. My walk with You is the most important thing in my life!! I pray, Lord, that You would once and for all rid me of those old feelings... or am I just confusing pure feelings of love for a person for more? I'm not used to expressing love in such a pure way."

One week later... *"This weekend some spiritual warfare was really going on in my head about (the same woman). I even dreamt about a relationship with her. Saturday morning I had doubts. I felt I might fall into sin, even though I know it's wrong. But I don't want these other feelings. Father, I pray that You will take them away for good. In the meantime, I know faith is not a feeling. Yesterday, reading Your Word, listening to Christian music and praying... as well as church today helped me immensely. Thank you, Lord! I know it's Your doing. Father, I just want to grow in my walk with You! I realize You are the only constant in my life. Thank You for loving me!"*

It is evident from these excerpts I truly believed "faith is not a feeling." I am so thankful I learned this truth early in my walk with Jesus. At this point, it's clear I was still struggling with same-sex attractions and feelings, but it was not my desire to act upon them. I knew God was changing me (1 Corinthians 6:11). I am not talking about the life-long change process that applies to every believer where God is conforming us into the image of His Son (Romans 8:29). The specific change I'm talking about here is to be truly heterosexual in thoughts, attractions, feelings and identity. I believed the feelings would eventually go away and that by the power of the Holy Spirit in me, I could keep from acting upon them (Romans 12:1-2; Galatians 5:16; 1 Corinthians 10:13). I recognized spiritual warfare coming from the devil, the father of lies (John 8:44); that he was bombarding my mind with fiery darts of doubt and fear causing me to think I might fall into sin. Therefore, I tried to refocus on the Lord, spend time with Him, desiring to stay surrendered to His working and His will for my life. I would sometimes find myself back on the throne of my life, but I loved Him (John 14:15) and wanted to be pleasing to Him and to allow Him to be in control of my life. These are the main truths from the Scriptures that I was choosing to believe and to live out:

Matthew 11:28 "'Come to Me!'" (Jesus speaking!)

1 Corinthians 6:11a "And such <u>were</u> some of you…"

1 Corinthians 6:18 "Flee sexual immorality."

Galatians 5:16 "Walk in the Spirit, and you shall not fulfill the lust of the flesh."

John 14:15 "'If you love Me, keep My commandments.'"

1 Corinthians 10:13b "…Who will not allow you to be tempted beyond what you are able, but with the temptation will also make the way of escape, that you may be able to bear it."

Romans 12:1b-2 "… Present your bodies [as] a living sacrifice, holy, acceptable to God, which is your reasonable service. And do not be conformed to this world, but be transformed by the renewing of your mind, that you may prove what is that good and acceptable and perfect will of God."

Proverbs 3:5 "Trust in the Lord with all your heart and lean not on your own understanding."

Now, surrendering goes without saying! If I were God, then I would have healed me of the attractions and feelings right away, but I'm not God, which is a very good thing! I trusted Him to heal me in His time. Let me make a very important point. For many people coming out of homosexuality, to be healed from same-sex attractions and feelings, they must understand how and why did they developed. I was different from most others in that I didn't have a real desire to understand how mine developed. We will, however, look at this issue later in the book. I just knew God would heal me and that was enough for me!

So, the critical point I want to make right now is this: every believer needs to fight the good fight of faith every day (1 Timothy 6:11; 1 Corinthians 9:26 & 27)! God has given us a battle plan in His Word: flee and pursue (2 Timothy 2:22). If we follow the battle plan, not allowing our feelings or circumstances to get in the way, then we will win the battle! What do we flee?

1. Flee immorality (1 Corinthians 6:18a)
2. Flee the world's influences (1 John 2:15-17)
3. Flee impure thoughts (Philippians 4:8)

For my coming out of homosexuality, this meant fleeing the gay scene altogether and separating myself from my old network of friends. The Bible puts it this way: "Come out from among them and be separate" (2 Corinthians 6:17). I wasn't going to go to gay bars or continue to participate in activities with all lesbian friends. If same-sex feelings or thoughts surfaced, then I couldn't dwell on them. I had to fill my mind with pure and edifying thoughts by reading God's Word; listening to worship and praise music and other edifying Christian music; reading Biblically-based Christian books; talking to and having fellowship with brothers and sisters in Christ, etc. I refused to be influenced any longer by those philosophies in the world that said homosexuality was a viable, loving lifestyle. I wanted Jesus and a life with Him, not the old lifestyle. Now please understand; it wasn't about fighting the good fight in my own strength; it was not disciplining my body through natural strength. Here is where the second part of the battle plan comes into play.

I needed to pursue, or put on, righteousness (Colossians 3:5-17), to pursue those things that would glorify the Lord. After I was born again, I began to pursue those things that would be pleasing to the Lord, and not pleasing to my flesh (Colossians 3:23)! How did I do that? God enabled me as I walked in the power of the Holy Spirit and thus received the fruit of self-control in my life (Galatians 5:16-17, 23)! And not only did I find I could deny my flesh, but by God's grace I received a precious gift. As I pursued those things that were pleasing to God, I found real contentment in my life (1 Timothy 6:6). Oh, the depths of God's love for me and for you!

For every child of God, this should be our battle plan, day-in and day–out. God will bless our obedience, our choosing to take Him at His Word! As I fought the good fight, I was able to deal with the same-sex attractions and feelings that continued to surface for a few years and then were gone. I was so blessed to be a new creature in Christ; I never had the desire to go back to the old life. Those attractions and feelings did not stumble me. I knew, and truly believed, I was a work in progress and that God had His reasons for not taking them away immediately! His ways are not our ways, and His ways are often times beyond our understanding. I made a decision not to lean on my own understanding, but instead, to trust in the Lord with all of my heart. You see, that's faith!

This understanding of faith and the desire to live out God's Word is essential for the person coming out of homosexuality; it is necessary for that real change to take place. But, even when a person has come out of homosexuality, is healed of their same-sex attractions and feelings and has acquired a completely heterosexual identity, there will still be temptations that will come our way where we are tempted to walk by our feelings, or by our circumstances, instead of by the truth of God's Word. This temptation is true for all believers. This point cannot be overemphasized! Our feelings are fickle; they can be tainted by our fleshly desires, the philosophies of the world and by the fiery darts that come from the devil that bombard our mind. Please understand; there is a battle going on for your soul! Taking God at His Word every single day is important in the life of a believer!

Therefore, dear reader, fight the good fight of faith. I challenge you to spend time daily in God's Word reading, studying, memorizing and meditating on it. Make it a practice to "flee and pursue." In the next chapter, we will look at other essential things that God wants us to pursue or put on! But as we close this chapter, let me ask you a very important question: How big is your God? Do you really believe that with Him all things are possible (Luke 18:27)? Keep on keeping on for Jesus, remembering that He will complete the work He has started in you (Philippians 1:6). Along the way, may this be your prayer (like it has been mine for many years): "Lord, increase my faith as I give You my life and walk in obedience to You. I want to be pleasing to You and to glorify you with my life. I continue to want you more than anything else in my life! In Jesus name, I pray. Amen."

"Love Flowed Down"

It was for me, the blood that You shed
It was for me, the cross that You bore
It was for me, the love that was poured
Down on Calvary

It was for me, the stripes on Your back
It was for me, the pain that You felt
It was for me, Your love that was poured
Down on Calvary, down on Calvary

Love flowed down from Your throne
Heals my body and my soul
Washes me and makes me whole
It was for me...

It was for me, death no longer reigns
It was for me, You rose from the grave
It was for me, the price that You paid
Down on Calvary, down on Calvary

Love flowed down from Your throne
Heals my body and my soul
Washes me and makes me whole
It was for me...

It was for me, that I could be free
It was for me, to live eternally
It was for me, that I could see
Love on Calvary, love on Calvary

Love flowed down from Your throne
Heals my body and my soul
Washes me and makes me whole
It was for me...

Free to live, for You alone
It was for me [1]

Chapter 4: One Thing Is Needful

W ithout a doubt, my changed life is the greatest proof that new birth has taken place in me. My new life started when I received Jesus (John 1:12) and consciously repented of my sin. I knew God was real and personal, the true and living God. To put it another way, I saw Jesus and began a personal relationship with Him which continues to this day. From the beginning, I understood I had the supernatural power of God in me to live my life in a manner pleasing to Him, but I would have to choose to obey the power of Jesus in me (1 John 3:9). That's where faith came in, choosing to trust God and live out His Word. From the very beginning, the true motivation for me to walk by the Spirit, and not by the desires of my flesh, has been God's love <u>for me</u>! I understood He even loved me when I was still doing my own thing! I was so grateful, and I felt I had been forgiven much.

Let me ask you this: is the cross personal to you? Perhaps you are not sure of what I mean. There is a wonderful song by Teresa Muller called "Love Flowed Down" which I have as the introduction to this chapter. Go back and read it again! As you read, ask yourself if the words of this song articulate your heart. All that He did… it was for me! That reality hit home in my heart when I was born again. Yes, God's love that poured down on Calvary freed me to live eternally for Him alone. I could see the love on Calvary… it was for me!

What difference did His personal love make in my life? All the difference in the world! Right from the very beginning, it was my desire to worship Him and live my life for Him. This kind of love I could not find in any homosexual relationship, nor in any earthly relationship, period! No other relationship could heal my soul. No other relationship could give me the deep inner-peace I received when I was born again. Even with the same-sex attractions and feelings hanging around for a few years, and the need for God to heal me of my tendency toward emotional dependency, I wanted and needed Jesus more than my old life! It was immediately the desire of my heart to flee the old lifestyle and pursue following Jesus!

Is the Lord truly personal to you? If you have never accepted the love of Calvary into your heart, then He cannot be personal to you. Only when we, sinful men and women, personally receive the love of God poured down at Calvary can we say… it was for me!

As I look back on what the Lord has done in my life over the years as He continues to work out His wonderful purpose and plan for my life, my love continues to grow toward Him! Oh, His love, it is for me! Motivated by His love toward me, I have continued to cultivate a heart after Him! I believe this is very important in the life of the believer. Why? How have I cultivated this heart after God? Well, that's what we will look at in this chapter, as we glean from the lives of King David, Mary of Bethany and Mary Magdalene. I will show you how the things we learn from their lives have applied to mine, and what their lives can mean to you.

First, let's look at the life of King David and his very personal relationship with God. In Psalm 63:1, David states this truth: "O God, You are my God." God was personal to him. He also knew God's love was better than life (Psalm 63:5). God's love motivated David to be a man after God's own heart (Acts 13:22). Through the many wonderful psalms that David wrote, we clearly see he loved God… worshipped God… and desired to please God. Why?

If we look at Psalm 103, I think we will find the answer. He starts the psalm by exhorting himself to give praise to the Lord with his whole being. Why? Well, he declares to God that he understands this reality: "You have not dealt with me according to my sins nor punished me according to my iniquities" (v. 11). David understands the reality that sin was the issue in his life. Then he states this truth: "So great is His mercy toward those who fear Him; as far as the east is from the west, so far has He removed our transgressions from us" (vv. 11b-12). David knew he had been forgiven much. He knew the basis for redemption and a renewed life was God's love. It was manifested to him through His abundant mercy that is from everlasting to everlasting (v. 17). David understood the benefits of God's love are for those who revere and worship God and live out His Word (v. 18). What should be our response to such love? David knew! "Bless the Lord, O my soul; and forget not all His benefits" (v. 2). How do we bless the Lord for all the mighty works He has done and continues to do in each of our lives? By continually lifting up our praise, thanksgiving and worship!

So, for me, as I live the new life God has given me, I can truly say His love toward me is better than my old life. I experienced God's love that flowed down on Calvary, and it was for me. Like David, I immediately had the desire to worship God for all He had done <u>for</u> me and for all He was beginning to do <u>in</u> me! I have continued to cultivate a heart after God, remembering the love on Calvary for me, because if I am not careful, my heart of worship toward God can wane.

What is the key to continuing to cultivate such a heart? Or to put it another way, what else did I learn early in my new life that would be the main ingredient in cultivating my love relationship with God, and cause it to grow deeper and deeper?

We can best see this lesson in the life of Mary of Bethany. In Luke 10:38-42, we have the story of two sisters, Mary and Martha. Jesus and the disciples have come for dinner. Mary is sitting at the feet of Jesus listening to Him; Martha is overextended with serving, and when she complains to the Lord, He softly rebukes her: "'Martha, Martha, you are worried and troubled about many things. But one thing is needed, and Mary has chosen that good part, which will not be taken away from her'" (v. 42).

In the Scriptures, Mary is always found sitting at the feet of Jesus. The lesson we learn is that Jesus needs to be our first priority. Nothing should come before Him. One thing is needful... Jesus. Mary was passionately devoted to Him. It's a heart issue. Mary and Martha both loved Jesus, but when Jesus was in her presence, it was Mary's priority to humble herself before Him and to listen intently to what He had to say, and not let anything distract her from doing just that. Are you devoted to Jesus? Is your relationship with Jesus your first priority every day? Do you protect that personal devotional time with Him so that you are not distracted from the most important thing you can do each day? For one thing is needful!

There was another Mary who was passionately devoted to Jesus: Mary Magdalene. She, too, loved the Lord and had a personal relationship with Him. There are two important things we glean from her relationship with the Lord. First of all, Mary wanted to be with Jesus! Mary was one of a group of prominent women who followed Him and helped meet His needs. Secondly, Mary loved Jesus by doing those things that pleased Him. When you read those parts of the Gospels that talk about Mary, you'll find the following to be true: she followed Him closely and listened to what He had to say as she ministered to Him; she loved those people He loved and gave generously to His work. This is how Mary manifested her love and passionate devotion to Jesus. Her devotion to Jesus resulted in submission to Him and living for Him. Everything she did, she did heartily as to the Lord (Colossians 3:23). In the life of Mary Magdalene, we see what a daily devotional life entails: walking with Him throughout the day; pleasing Him; loving those people He loves; and doing His will for our life.

So, how do the lives of Mary of Bethany and Mary Magdalene relate to my new life? First of all, right from the very beginning, I had a true, personal relationship with the Lord where love prevailed. I understood that He first loved me when I was still a mess and living my life for myself. When I personally received the love He poured down on Calvary, it lead to repentance, and I sensed such an absolute unworthiness to receive such a wonderful gift, but receive it I did. I understood my utter helplessness to clean up the mess of my old life by myself. The deep joy and inner-peace I immediately received in my soul was proof of God's personal love for me. I was so grateful, knowing I was forgiven so much. Therefore, from the beginning, because of what He had done for me personally, my heart's desire was to worship the Lord, and I did! From the beginning, I was blessed to fellowship at a church that places an emphasis on worship through song and the teaching of God's Word. I pursued a personal relationship with Jesus, and like Mary Magdalene, it was my heart's desire to do those things that pleased Jesus.

From the very beginning, the foundation for a quality-time of fellowship with Jesus was the Word of God. This cannot be emphasized enough! In order to know what to flee from and what to pursue (what I spoke about in the last chapter), I needed to be in His Word. To grow in my relationship with God, it was imperative to know Him and to understand His nature and His character, and that knowledge and understanding comes through reading His Word. To know God's will for my life and how to please Him, I had to read and study the Bible. And of course, my relationship with the Lord was a two-way street right from the beginning: I learned about Him through His Word, and I shared my heart with Him through prayer.

With some journal excerpts, let me show you that I understood from early on that "one thing is needful."

January 8, 1990: *"I love You, and praise You, and need You in my life. I thank You for the change in my lifestyle."* This wish can be found time and time again. He was the one needful thing in my life and the One responsible for the wonderful changes taking place in my life.

Like Mary Magdelene, it was my heart's desire to live for Jesus. In other words, this is not how I felt! "Oh well, I suppose I must devote my life to God?" Oh, no! The reality of God's love poured down on

Calvary was personal... it was for me! Thank you, Jesus! Therefore, I ministered my love to Him by making Him the priority of my life and living to please Him.

March 25, 1990: *"Father, another week has gone by, and it was very busy due to the start of new classes and my new responsibility of working with a student teacher. Father, I found strength in You. Patience and self-control were evident all week. Thank You, Lord! I started each day with a quiet time reading Your Word and praying. I tried to focus on You all week and do Your will, not mine. It was good to go to Bible study Wednesday evening. I am so thankful for the guidance of the Holy Spirit all week... This weekend has been a time spent thinking about You; reading Your Word; reading another Christian book about not trusting emotions; listening to Christian music... spending much time with You. I pray I can know Your will for my life and what gifts You have given me, Lord Jesus. I pray You will use me big-time."*

It was my desire to follow Him closely and pursue knowing Him. Like Mary of Bethany, it was my priority to daily sit at the feet of Jesus and listen to Him through His Word; to share my heart with Him through prayer; and worship Him through song and prayer because I felt He was worthy of my continuous praise and worship. A huge desire to serve Him was growing in me.

Now, does this mean that I always sat at His feet when I should? No, the cares of the world and the circumstances of my life would cause me to take my eyes off of Jesus and put them on myself, a fact which this journal excerpt can attest to:

March 17, 1991: *"Lord, just thank you for church today to get my head together after the past week. Boy, a couple mornings I had little or no devotional time and no prayer time at night and the enemy really got to me, making my temperament so up and down all week. I'm not going to go without my devotions, prayer time and time with believers... I didn't go to any Bible studies and the singles thing fell through. Thank You for speaking to me through Pastor Dwight's message today. To keep from getting caught up in fleshly and worldly things, I need to watch and pray so I will not fall into temptation. The spirit is willing, but the flesh is weak (Matthew 26:41). ... I've had these dreams about getting into a physical relationship with them. My spirit wants to do what is right, but my flesh is weak. Lord, I pray for Your strength in me; Father, I am Yours. I do not want to lead my old lifestyle... please take away any homosexual desires. I will persevere through these dreams... with Your strength. I look to You, give it to You. Thank you, Father! I am also reminded I need to stay close to good Christians. Father, I love You and praise You! In Jesus name, amen!"*

How important it is to keep focused on Jesus and to cultivate a close relationship with Him! Can you see the importance of God's Word in my life? As I continued to study God's Word, I became aware of so many precious promises of God that gave me hope! Even though dealing with same-sex feelings and these dreams, I knew Who my strength was in, and in no way did I want to lead the old lifestyle any longer!

The longer I walk with the Lord, and through the trials of life and the living-out of God's Word, the more I have grown in my devotion to God. My love for the Lord continues to deepen, and I can truly say I am passionately devoted to Him. I know how needy I am for Jesus every single day; for without Him, I can do nothing, but with Him in control of my life, by the power of the Spirit, I can do all things! How did I get to this place? By making my relationship with God my first priority, and thus spending time with Him daily in prayer and by listening to Him through His Word so that my mind is renewed daily. Like Mary Magdalene, my desire to love the Lord and be pleasing to Him gave me the motivation to do His will for my life and to love those Jesus loves.

Now, at this point I need to say something. I'm grieved when I see how churches and believers are moving away from listening to God through His Word. It is the spirit, truth and life for the believer. The whole counsel of God is being replaced with man's philosophy. How would listening to man's philosophy have affected my new life in Christ? Quite likely, I would not have succeeded in coming out of the lesbian lifestyle.

Without the Bible, I would not have understood that I was a sinner who needed a Savior. I would not have understood homosexuality is a sinful lifestyle. Pursuing a righteous life would have been impossible. I would not have grown in faith, because faith comes by hearing and hearing by the Word of God (Romans

10:17). I would not be able to live a life pleasing to God in all areas of my life because without faith, it is impossible to please God. I would not know my God like I do. How could I have a passionate love relationship with Someone I do not know? The same-sex attractions and feelings quite likely would have caused me to stumble because I would not have known the Bible says the homosexual can change, and I would have walked by the feelings, allowing Satan to deceive me into thinking that being a lesbian is who I am. God would not have had the opportunity to completely restore my heterosexual female identity (this is something I will talk about in the next chapter). I would not have known and believed the wonderful promise that He who began a good work in me would be faithful to complete it (Philippians 1:8).

God has truly completed a work in my soul so that I am the woman He created me to be with heterosexual attractions, feelings and identity. I'm still, of course, in a process of change where I am being made more and more like Jesus. But I am confident of this! Just as I have come out of the homosexual lifestyle and been healed of my same-sex attractions, so can any other struggler who seeks true change. Remember the love of Calvary: it was for me and it was for you, but you must receive it. The love of Jesus truly has changed my life, and it can change your life, too. The things I learned early in my walk that helped me come out of the homosexual lifestyle and be completely healed can do the same for anyone because they are based on God's Word. The truth in God's Word does not change. There are some who would say the Bible is an outdated book and no longer relevant for daily living. To that claim, I would simply but emphatically say, "Nonsense!" I have found it quite relevant to meet all my needs.

This I can tell you with all confidence because I have experienced it in my life, as have thousands of other ex-gays; true change can come for anyone struggling with same-sex attractions and for anyone who has been living in bondage to the homosexual lifestyle. One thing is needful! Lasting change comes through a person... Jesus Christ. It's truly a heart issue! If you have not personally received the love of Calvary, won't you bow your knee now, and then seek to live a life of simple devotion to Jesus? I can promise you that with Jesus and His Word as the foundation of your new life, and if you will be diligent to put into practice the things I have learned that I am sharing in this book, true change will take place in your life. And like me, you will want to proclaim, to God be the glory!

Journal:

March 17, 1991: *"Thank You for the message today at church. To keep from getting caught up in fleshly lusts and worldly things, I need to "watch and pray so I will not fall into temptation. The spirit is willing, but my flesh is weak" (Matthew 26:41). I've had these dreams about getting into a physical relationship with them (two girl students). My spirit wants to do what is right, but my flesh is weak. Lord, I pray for Your strength in me... Father, I am Yours... I do not want to lead my old lifestyle. Please, Lord Jesus, take any temptation away from me. Take away any homosexual attraction feelings. I pray You would use me and that I will be who You want me to be! I will persevere through these dreams...in Your strength. I look to You... give it to You. I also was reminded I need to stay in close fellowship with good Christians."* (Note: This is the last time I struggled with dreams of this nature!)

Scriptures:

Genesis 1:27 "So God created man in His own image; in the image of God He create him; **male** <u>and</u> **female** He created them." (Emphasis mine)

Philippians 1:6 "Being confident of this very thing, that He who has begun a good work in you **will complete it** until the day of Jesus Christ." (Emphasis mine)

Chapter 5: Restoring Sexual Identity

As I have revealed in my testimony in chapter 1, same-sex attractions first surfaced in my life for my best friend in junior high, and they would continue to come and go through college. Then, two years out of college when I had same-sex attractions for a friend on my summer recreational softball team, I not only chose to act upon them, but I chose to lead the homosexual lifestyle which would last for over 15 years. On the surface, I told myself I was born a homosexual, but deep down in my soul, I knew that was not true. Before long, I developed a lesbian identity; my partner and I moved to Florida where we exclusively acquired homosexual friends and began socializing at gay bars. It was exciting to go to these places where we could drink alcohol, dance, have wonderful romantic dinners and watch drag shows. We began to socialize at homes, with alcohol as a huge part of every gathering. I often had lustful attractions for other women, even though I tried to remain committed to my partner. After two years, we moved back to Wisconsin, and my last 10 years in the lifestyle I rarely went to gay bars, but I attended lesbian parties and gatherings. I spent my recreational time with gay **and** straight friends. During this period of time, I also had an attraction toward a male colleague at the school where I was teaching. We were close to having an affair, but we never did. I began to spend more time with straight friends and colleagues, especially after the last woman I was with broke-up with me. Then, when I was born again, I left my network of gay friends. I learned God's wisdom as I read in His Word; I "[came] out from among them" (2 Corinthians 6:17). I wanted Jesus more than the old lifestyle, so I was not going to play with fire. I did not want to give the lusts of my flesh an opportunity to kick in; I did not want to succumb to temptation. I immediately began to replace my gay friends with godly Christian friends, women and men from church, and about three years after I was born again, the same-sex attraction and feelings went away. Initially, my friend Jill came along side and discipled me through phone calls, letters and visits. She and the women I developed friendships with at church were important, godly female role models that I wanted to emulate and identify with. This identification was important as I had spent 15 years identifying with lesbian women. The proper sexual identity needed to be restored so I could be the woman God wanted me to be.

There are those who think trying to change the homosexual is harmful and impossible. In her book <u>Restoring Sexual Identity</u>, Anne Paulk presents the following question and answer:

"Are women stuck in their sexuality? After talking to hundreds of women during the past several years and hearing their stories of same-sex attraction, I'm convinced the answer to this first important question is no. Some of the women I've talked to have admitted to being attracted to women most of their lives. But I also talked to women who have been married and otherwise hetero-sexual, yet have found themselves in homo-sexual relationships. Still others have shared their stories of childhood experimentation with other girls..." [1]

A woman's sexuality can change; meaning a woman who is attracted to women can change and be attracted to men. It is also true that a man attracted to men can change and be attracted to women. The ex-gay ministries have found this to be true for thousands of people coming out of homosexuality. Perhaps you find that hard to believe.

Well, it may be helpful at this time to ask and answer a very important question. Where does same-sex attraction come from? Is a person born gay and that's the reason for these usually unwanted feelings? I am not going to go into the results of all the major scientific studies done to determine if homosexuality is inborn. You can do your homework, and check out some of the resources I have noted in this book, and find the results to various important studies. But in one sentence I can tell you what you will find: there is no scientific evidence that a man or woman is born a homosexual. I wanted to believe I was born that way because it provided an explanation for why I had these attractions. It helped quiet the inner protest in my soul that said it was wrong. I thought, "How can God condemn me for simply being the way I was created? Wasn't homosexuality just another way to love, and didn't I hear somewhere that God is a God of love?"

Well, if I was not born with same-sex attractions, then, it must be a choice, right? Well, yes and no! Hang in here with me while we reason this out. If we are all born to be heterosexual, did you choose to be heterosexual, to have opposite-sex attractions? I mean, did you make a logical choice like: I want to be a teacher; or I will only buy GM cars; or I want to invest in a home and no longer rent. No, being a heterosexual and having opposite-sex attractions is not a choice you make. God's plan for human sexuality (Genesis 1:27-28; 2:18-25) took its natural course, and when your hormones kicked in, you found yourself attracted to the opposite sex. In a distorted way, the same event takes place in the person with same-sex attractions, though it is unnatural. When I began to have same-sex attractions for my girl friend, was it a choice I made? Did I wake up one morning and say I want to have same-sex attractions for my girl friend? The answer is no! What happened was it happened; these unwanted, but very real, same-sex attractions and feeling occurred. The attractions and feelings were not a choice on my part, but when I chose to act upon them, it was then that choice came into play. Choice further came into play when I eventually chose to lead the lifestyle for 15 years.

So, where do these very real same-sex attractions and desires come from? They develop unnaturally due to certain environmental factors in a person's developmental years. In talking to thousands of people seeking a way out of homosexuality, the ex-gay ministries have found that a strong combination of common environmental factors, along with the person's own make-up (such as temperament, interests, and abilities) greatly contribute to the development of same-sex attractions. The combination is not the same for everyone. The most common factors are:

- Early childhood development: such as the development of atypical play patterns; breakdown of bonding with the same-sex parent; damaged or unhealthy parent-child relationship leading to gender role rejection; or emotional detachment from the same-sex parent.
- Family background: such as the absence of a parent.
- Peer pressure: especially peer-rejection.
- Childhood trauma: such as sexual abuse or extreme emotional abuse.

Shortly after I was born again, my friend Jill sent me the chapter of a book [2] dealing with two lesbians who were born again. It explained how these factors had influenced each of them. It gave me enough information so that I understood how same-sex feelings developed; and for me, that was all I needed to know. There were two important reasons I did not feel the need to figure out specifically what combination of factors during my developmental years had caused me to develop these attractions. First of all, I did not suffer from abuse when I was growing up. That is unusual, as 85-90% of lesbians have been sexually abused, and about 75% of gay men have been abused. The second reason was that I had no doubt my parents loved me, so I simply did not want to try to figure out why I personally developed same-sex attractions! In my thinking, this is a parental blame–game (though that is not the case). Instead, I was satisfied to give God time to heal me of them and restore my identity as a heterosexual woman.

But for the majority of those people coming out of homosexuality after the person is born again, male or female, an understanding of the development of same-sex attractions leading to homosexual behavior and identity helps point the way to true resolution and healing. They can look back and see what they are responsible for and what they are not responsible for. When God brings to light their own wrong actions and attitudes, they can confess their guilt to God and confess all their wrong choices and receive His forgiveness. When a person has been the victim of circumstances and the hurtful actions of other people (as in the case of abuse), they can gain understanding and learn to forgive.

God will hold the homosexuals responsible for their own choices and actions. It's important to keep in mind that while these factors influence the development of same-sex attractions, in some cases, it is one's perception of childhood. For example, growing up, a child may have felt a lack of love from a particular parent, but that may not be reality. That particular parent may have loved them very much. Sometimes perceptions are false but still influence the development of the child.

Recently, with a better understanding of all these things, for ministry purposes, I determined to take the time to discern the primary factors that, along with my make-up, most contributed to my development of same-sex attractions. Two factors stood out immediately. First of all, in my early childhood development I experienced atypical play patterns for a girl. Secondly, my personal make-up was such that my interests and abilities fit right in with the environmental factors that greatly influenced my development. I grew up in a neighborhood with only boys as friends. I was a tomboy as far back as I can remember. I had very good athletic ability. I was as good as or better than the boys in all the sports and the activities we played, both in my neighborhood and in gym class during elementary school. I was always respected and liked by the boys, and I was very comfortable having them as friends. I developed the same interests as the boys and became very competitive in everything I did. During this time, I also took great pleasure in knowing how to start the lawnmowers when my older brother often could not. I enjoyed mowing the lawn and making things with hammers, saws and nails. I preferred doing things that were my dad's tasks than those things that were my mom's household tasks.

As a little girl, my favorite TV shows were westerns such as Roy Rodgers and Gene Autry. I had gun and holster sets and cowgirl outfits. I enjoyed playing and pretending that I was a cowboy in the Wild West more than playing with the few dolls I had. As I shared in my testimony, during my elementary years, when my neighborhood friends and I used our imaginations to act out these TV westerns, as well as detective shows and the like, I often played the part of a man.

It is interesting, however, that during this period of time I did have a cousin that I spent time with, and we enjoyed watching American bandstand; reading movie star and teen magazines; and going to movies. We kept up with what was going on in the Hollywood, movie and music scenes, as well as the fashions for teens, even before we were teens. I believe this prepared me for my switch of interests in junior high, which really came out of necessity to be one of the girls. And throughout junior and senior high school, when I was best friends with one of the most popular girls in our class, I was part of that popular group, at least on the fringe! I felt my popularity was not on my own merits, however, but only because I was her friend. Remember, I had been the best at everything I did in my early years with the boys and was appreciated and respected. This period of time translated into rejection, really. I was not as comfortable and confident talking with my peers in high school as I had been in the earlier years. I was highly respected by the girls for one thing, for being the best in physical education classes and GAA (Girls Athletic Association) Sports, which were very popular with the "in-crowd" girls. In sports I was in my element and really enjoyed the accolades. My girl friend was good in this area as well, but I was better!

As I have shared in my testimony, a huge problem developed in our relationship. Besides the fact that we acted upon the same-sex feelings that developed in junior high, she was very controlling, and I became very emotionally-dependent on her, which, in later years, would be a huge part of my lesbian relationships. You must understand; I still wanted to have boy friends and not just have a relationship with my girl friend. During this period of time, two more things stand out. First, when my girl friend wanted to get together with me, she usually came before any of my boyfriends. Second, throughout those years, my mom stressed again and again that I needed to be the one to say "no" when dating so as not to get pregnant. I developed a tremendous fear of getting pregnant, and I thought that men just viewed women as sex objects, neither a valued partner nor sexually-appealing in a positive sense. Remember, I had a long relationship with a young man in college and "saying no" was always on my mind; it became very difficult, but I never gave in. Remember, I was not doing this to be pleasing to God, but because of extreme fear!

So, during my college days when the same sex-feelings surfaced with much more frequency, I began to value to a greater degree my relationships with women because I felt loved, valued and appreciated and did not have to worry about getting pregnant. I felt such an emotional attachment with the women in these same-sex relationships where no fear was involved. Well, almost no fear; there was always the fear of people finding out I was having a relation-ship with a woman. This was actually a good fear that never went away until I accepted Christ!

This is the combination of environmental/devel-opmental factors that I believe lead to my same-sex attractions and feelings, and eventually lead to acquiring a lesbian identity. But, in my case, it was not a deeply-seated identity. Therefore, when I was born again, it did not take God long to restore proper female sexuality in me and to heal me of same-sex feelings. Oh, how grateful I am.

Here are the two key truths in this chapter that any struggler in this area or anyone desiring to help a person struggling needs to glean. The first truth is this: we were all created male and female, in the image of God (Genesis 1:27). This is our true iden-tity. I am a female God created, but due to a specific strong combination of environmental/developmental factors in my life and my own make-up, I developed same-sex attractions and then made a choice to act upon them. I was not born a homosexual. Just as the Scriptures say, homosexuality is a behavior that is a sin. My behavior turned into a lifestyle when I chose to live it for 15 years.

The second truth is this: These same-sex attraction feelings took time to develop, and when a person is born again, they usually do not go away immediately. But, this is where faith comes into play. "He who began the work will be faithful to complete it" (Philippians 1:6). This verse gave me great hope very soon after I was born again. Oh, the importance of knowing and believing the wonderful promises from the Word of God. These unwanted, unnatural attractions and feelings will go away as they did in me.

So, restoring proper sexual identity and feelings will take time. It is critically important during this time that the new believer coming out of homosexuality have quality fellowship with other believers. In the book <u>Coming Out of Homosexuality</u>, the authors state this important truth: *"Nearly all the ex-gays we know have made this difficult transition with the strong support of Christian friends. Most of these significant friendships have formed through local church involvement."* [3]

For those of you reading this book who are coming out of homosexuality, I urge you to take this seriously and seek fellowship. To all other brothers and sisters in Christ I urge you to make yourselves available! Perhaps you may even take it to another level and form a friendship with a person coming out of homosexuality. Along with fellowship, the young believer must acquire godly friends for a support system as they begin to separate themselves from their gay friends, and perhaps even leave their lover.

This can be a very difficult time of loss and grieving even though it is the right thing to do.

I was extremely blessed to have both good fellowship and develop good friends. And God used my new special friendship with Jill in so many ways, but specifically, He used our friendship to address emotional dependency issues that surfaced in our friendship on my part, even though it was not a lesbian relationship. God used our friendship to begin to heal me of those emotional dependency issues. I had developed too much of a dependency on Jill, and I first needed to understand there was such a thing as emotional dependency and then I needed to be freed from its grip on me. This was a work God would have to do in my life. In my case, this healing process would take longer than anything else. This is what we need to look at in the next chapter!

Journal:

October 18, 1990: *"I must identify myself with God's interest in other people, not my interests. The key to devotion is being attached to nothing and no one, saving the Lord Himself. The loyalty of a missionary is to keep his soul open to the nature of Christ. Lord, I want to be like You and to think like You think."*

April 1, 1991: *"Lord, my reading today in A.W. Tozer's <u>The Pursuit of God</u>, was so enlightening and convicting. Father, I do want to know You more, but I need to possess nothing. I want You to be able to work in me. I pray You will have Your rightful place in my heart, instead of things or people before You. Lord, I come trembling, but I do come. Lord, I commit all things to You. I just want to be who You want me to be."*

December 29, 1991: *"Yesterday's Oswald Chambers' devotion was based on Matthew 18:3: '"Truly, truly I say to you, unless you are converted and become like little children, you shall not enter the kingdom of heaven."' I've always thought of conversion as a one-time event. Chambers talks about continuous conversion… the relationship of the natural life to the spiritual life is one of continuous conversion, and it's something we sometimes object to. How true! Our natural life must not rule; You must rule in us. What You call obstinate weakness, we call strength. How true! There are areas of our lives which have not yet been brought into subjection, and it can only be done by continuous conver-*

sion. Lord, I ask that You'd show me any area in my life that I have not given to You! Father, continue to make my heart pure... whiter than snow."

Chapter 6: Dependency: Good or Bad

As we begin this chapter, it is important that we keep it in the context of key truths we have gleaned in the previous chapters. There is hope for the person struggling with same-sex attraction and for the person desiring to come out of the homosexual lifestyle. It comes in a person: Jesus Christ. The good news is that through Christ, God has made a way for us to be given a new life. Our part is to put up the white flag of surrender and **allow Jesus to meet our deepest needs**. By faith we live out His Word and do not walk by feelings, especially when our feelings are in opposition to God's Word. For example, God created everyone male or female. God's plan for healthy sexuality is between a man and a woman. The truth is this: No one is born a homosexual. It is essential to understand that the very real, unwanted same-sex attraction feelings developed due to environmental factors and the person's own make-up. Then, when we chose to act upon those feelings and to live homosexuality as a lifestyle, a homosexual identity becomes more and more ingrained in us. But, by the grace of God and in His time, with Jesus the center of our lives, He will restore opposite-sex attraction feelings and a heterosexual identity. God will change us if we trust Him and will ourselves to do His will.

For the Christian, life becomes a process of learning to live by the power of Jesus Christ in us. Change is a process, part of the sanctification process all Christians experience. However, for the person coming out of homosexuality, if change is our only motivation and not the Lord, we may not be successful, or at the very least, we may struggle and fall away for awhile. But when we trust God to complete the work He has started in us, He will restore and make up for the destruction and abuse of our previous years.

Yes, God is the great Restorer! I have experienced this to be true in my own life. I was not saved until I was 39, and I often think, "What wasted years!" Yet, one of the most exciting promises in the Bible for anyone who has undergone extreme emotional pain or loss, as well as a seemingly wasted life is found in Joel 2:25-26. God says to His devastated people, including you and me:

> "'So I will restore to you the years that the swarming locust has eaten, the crawling locust, the consuming locust, and the chewing

locust, My great army which I sent among you. You shall eat in plenty and be satisfied, and praise the name of the LORD your God, Who has dealt wondrously with you; and My people shall never be put to shame.'"

God restores us, and God gives us new life, so our dependency must be on God. He will meet our greatest needs, and He will also put people in our lives for the purpose of meeting other needs, as well as to bless us! He has created us for relationships, but our relationship with Him must have precedence over all others. In all areas of our life we must learn to be needy for God. God will reveal to us those areas of our life we are trying to live out in our own strength. Our total dependency on God is not weakness, but indeed, great strength. When we are weak in ourselves, then we are strong in Him (2 Corinthians 13:9). We must be dependent on Him for all things! We abide in Jesus because without Him we can do nothing (John 15:5). But, with Him, we can do all things (Philippians 4:13).

Remember, God is the giver of all good things in our life, and first and foremost among those good things is His Son! We need to be dependent on God... not people! Worship God, not another person. In Romans 1:21-25, we are told the first step leading to homosexuality is worshiping the created thing rather than the Creator. We are really wading into quicksand when we look at another person to be what God should be in our lives. When we are dependent on another person in this manner, it is typically called emotional dependency. Depending on and worshiping another person as the answer to all our needs could also be called friendship idolatry. Idolatry is a sin; no relationship should take God's place!

Why such an emphasis on dependency issues, you ask? For many coming out of homosexuality, emotional dependency is often the central struggle in the healing process and one of the toughest issues to deal with. This should not be surprising because at its root, homosexuality is **not** sexual. Gay and lesbian feelings point to deeper emotional needs. Homosexual desires and feelings, at their core, develop from **unmet emotional needs**. Emotional dependency was at the center of all of my lesbian relationships. Emotional dependency occurs when the **ongoing presence** and **nurturing** of another person is perceived to be necessary for the basic needs of love and personal security to be met. The nurturing might come in many different forms, such as attentiveness, listening, admiration, counsel, affirmation and time spent together. Now, these forms of nurturing are not bad, and we do them in relationships. Emotional dependency occurs when a person thinks that this nurturing must come from the nurturer on an ongoing basis, and the nurturer alone becomes the needy person's security. In a dependent relationship, one or both people are looking to **a person** to meet their basic needs for love and security rather than **to Christ.** When your worth, peace of mind, inner stability and happiness are anchored on a person and on that person's response to you, you are emotionally-dependent. So here's the problem. We will remain prone to dependency unless the underlying **spiritual** and **emotional** problems are resolved.

What might be some of the red flags that emotional dependency exists in a relationship? When either person:

- Experiences <u>frequent</u> jealousy, possessiveness and a desire for exclusivity, and views other people as a <u>threat</u> to the relationship
- <u>Prefers</u> to spend time alone with this friend and becomes frustrated when this does not happen
- Becomes <u>irrationally</u> angry or depressed when the other withdraws slightly
- Loses interest in other friendships
- Experiences romantic or sexual feelings leading to fantasy toward this person
- Becomes <u>preoccupied</u> with the other person's appearance, personality, problems and interests
- Is <u>unwilling</u> to make short or long-range plans that do not include the other person [1]

So, what are a few of the most likely spiritual and emotional problems behind these actions? First of all, spiritually, there might be an element of covetousness that causes a person to desire to possess a person God has not given to them. Another spiritual problem I have already mentioned could be idolizing another person, making them the center of your life when it should be God. A person could also be simply rebelling against God and refusing to surrender areas of their lives to God. Lastly, a person may lack trust in God and does not believe He will meet their needs if they do things His way.

Emotional problems from within our soul may stem from hurts from our past that leave us with the need to be affirmed and accepted, and therefore, we might have feelings of rejection and a deep, unmet need for love. We may harbor bitterness and resentment towards those who have hurt us. If we were abandoned by an important person in our lives, then we may feel we have to control relationships so as not to have that person abandon us. In all of these situations, we leave ourselves open to emotionally-dependent relationships. When we come to understand the hurts behind our emotional dependency, we need to express our pain and inner turmoil to God. Then, through confession and prayer, both in our quiet times with the Lord and with other believers, healing can take place. We must trust God in and with our relationships!

When I began to research this area for Bridge of Hope Ministry, and more specifically for writing this book, I knew emotional dependency had been a problem since my relationship with my best friend in high school and had existed in all of my lesbian relationships. Then after I was born again, this problem soon surfaced in my new, growing friendship with Jill. While we have never talked about it, because of the resources she gave me, I know Jill recognized I had become way more dependent on her than I should be. When I was about a year and half old in the Lord, she gave me Dee Brestin's book The Friendships of Women [2] (from which came the chapter that I mentioned in chapter 5). I read the whole book and learned what is involved in a healthy friendship. I read again how emotional dependency was an issue in the relationship of the two lesbians, and also how it can be a growing cancer in the friendships of women if it is not recognized and dealt with in a godly manner.

When I look back in my earliest journal, I can discern dependency problems in my friendship with Jill. Let's look at a few excerpts from my journal:

January 8, 1990: *"Lord, I also continue to miss Jill and have these mixed emotions (**love to anger**) that she is not in touch, etc. Lord, please help me to **love unconditionally** and guide me in our friendship so I know whether I should leave things be for awhile… or should I write or call her. Help me know what to do!"*

May 14, 1990: *"I am better able to **love Jill unconditionally**. Lord, I pray for further improvement in this area."*

I felt that continuous nurturing by Jill was necessary in my life. When she went into full-time ministry, Jill could not be in touch or visit as often as she had, which meant I could no longer receive on an on-going basis the personal counsel, affirmation and love that she had given me. I missed her, but I was putting the condition on our relationship that she should still continue to put the same amount of time in our relationship, even in this new season in her life. So, I would often pray, "Lord, help me to love Jill unconditionally." I knew the swing of emotions from love to anger was a sign of the unfair expectations I was putting on our friendship. I did not really know how to deal with these emotions, nor did I understand the unmet needs behind these emotions.

June 24, 1990: *"Reading Dee Brestin's book <u>The Friendships of Women</u>[3], that Jill gave me recently has helped me to **understand** even more the wonderful **friendship** You have blessed us with."*

What I did not express in this excerpt, but what I knew to be true, was that God had convicted me of some things that were not right in our friendship... things on my part! But it wasn't until I read the booklet on emotional dependency that Jill gave to me that I was convicted of the fact that I was too dependent on Jill. Yet, instead of dealing with the dependency, I put the booklet away and tried to ignore what it showed me to be. She was not emotionally-dependent on me, but was trying to help me through these materials. We should have discussed the issue, but we never did. I should have confided my struggle with one of my other godly friends to help me work through this and hold me accountable. She let more and more time elapse between calls and letters. I needed God's help, so He put boundaries in our friendship by leading her to do this. God was beginning to work, but this healing would take much more time than it would take healing from same-sex attraction feelings. Here are a few more journal excerpts:

August 11, 1990: *"Lord, forgive me for my sinful feelings in recent days concerning my friends. I've felt a little **jealousy, resentment,** and **anger** for the following reasons: Jill has not gotten in touch; Sarah has not put much into our friendship; and Sue and*

*Jim don't call. Father, I pray that I can love uncondi-
tionally, my friends and You. Help me to do my part
in those friendships, and guide me and help me to
leave it up to my friends to follow Your guidance in
doing their part. Father, **help me** not to try to **control**
these situations. I give them to you because I know I
will just make a mess of things. Thank You for Your
love and all the blessings I have received from You,
Father!"*

August 13, 1990: *"I haven't heard from Jill yet.
Father, I pray I can **'feel' Your unfailing love** when
I am **feeling alone.** I have faith You always love me
and do what is best… but I don't know that I really
feel that love. **Am I supposed to?"***

There are two very obvious things going on here.
I asked God to help me so I would not try to control
these relationships, which reveals that I understood
God was in the process of healing me. An emotionally-dependent person will often try to control the
relationship through manipulation, and I did not
want to do that, though I was tempted to do so by
this fleshly desire. I knew this was not the godly way
to act, and it would only make things worse in those
relationships. So, as a young Christian and with no
support of another godly person, whether it be a
pastor or a friend, I committed these relationships to
God as best I knew how.

The second thing going on here was that I was
"feeling alone." At this point in my relationship with
God, I knew that ultimately I needed to be dependent
on Him for all things and that somehow He would
meet all my needs. I understood God's unconditional

love for me, but I wanted to feel His love for me because the reality was, I was lonely. Then I asked a very important question. Am I supposed to feel lonely? I wanted the loneliness to go away, but I had no one to talk to about these relationship issues, especially since they related to emotional dependency. Jill and I didn't talk about these issues, but I believe that would have helped a great deal.

Finally, I got to the place where I was able to accept my friendship with Jill the way it was. I loved her and considered her a very important person in my life, and I always will. But the key was, I felt no anger, resentment, etc. I just gave her to God, and then I realized I was no longer struggling in anyway with this issue in our relationship. As a Christian, I have had consistent fellowship with people at church and developed other good friends. It's interesting that all these other friendships I have acquired since I was born again have been healthy, with no emotional dependency at the core.

Here is what I really want to share concerning this issue. I believe if I had shared with someone early on about this issue and been accountable, I don't think it would have taken almost 19 years to finally be able to say I was healed. How did God show me I was healed? Through a wonderful, new, close friendship with my friend, Ellen. After 14 or 15 years of walking with the Lord, and many years of teaching Bible studies and being involved in Women's Ministry, I was becoming a close friend with another wonderful sister in Christ, a friendship which surely was a gift from God. One day I was in the car with another close sister in Christ, and I said, "You know, God is using my new friendship with Ellen to show me He has healed me of emotional dependency." Then a year and a half after that conversation, while writing this book, I got an email from Ellen. I'd like to share portions of it with you:

> *"I wanted to ask the expert on dependency issues a question. How do you know if there are unhealthy dependency issues going on in a relationship? There's been a nagging in my heart about boundaries that is not going away. I've prayed about it and want to talk with you about it... To be truthful I'm a bit concerned about us. Please don't take this the wrong way, but we seem to be bordering on becoming emotional partners because we talk once or several times a day (internet of course), and it seems if we don't, then something's wrong... I've never been like this before, and it feels uncomfortable. I need your take on this. You know more than I do about these things. I want you to pray about this and ask the Lord what's going on. Ask Him if there is anything unhealthy in our relationship... if there is emotional dependency going on... I had a friend who was married, had three great kids. She was very spiritual. She met a lady back east doing ministry... well, over time they became involved. They hid it from their husbands... I just want to be healthy, pleasing to God and not give the*

devil a foothold in any area, and since I've been feeling a bit uncomfortable, I wanted to talk with you about it..."

My immediate reaction was disbelief as I did not see this issue coming, but I also felt fear and panic that our wonderful friendship would end. I felt some insecurity about our relationship, not trusting that she really wanted to keep it. I did not get irrationally angry and want to manipulate the situation, which would have been a clear sign of emotional dependency on my part. I took it to God in prayer. The feelings did not go away immediately, however. It was all I could think about for the next 24 hours, so I continued to pray, asking God to search my heart and to show me how to respond.

I prayerfully evaluated our friendship according to the truths listed earlier in this chapter and all I knew about emotional dependency. For example, had either of us experienced **frequent** jealousy, possessiveness, etc.? The answer was "no." There had been times I experienced jealousy, but it had all been taken to God and dealt with. Had either of us become irrationally angry or depressed when the other withdrew slightly? The key word is **irrationally**, and the answer was "no." There had not been any romantic or sexual feelings on my part toward her and vice versa. I also prayerfully skimmed over portions of other resources I have already mentioned that applied to establishing healthy relationships, especially close friendships after coming out of homosexuality and emotionally-dependent relationships.

Well, it actually took a week to sort through every-thing with the Lord's help. There were some emails back and forth and also a couple days of silence on Ellen's part that God used to work in me. During this time, God showed me so much that I would not have seen had I decided to walk by the lusts of my flesh and my feelings. I was going through a time of extreme temptation and testing (we will look at spiri-tual warfare in an upcoming chapter), but it was my desire to be honest with God and walk by the Spirit, to ask for discernment to know what thoughts were from God and what thoughts were from the enemy of my soul.

Let me share with you my heart during this time and what the Lord was showing me as I recorded it in my journal March 15, 2007:

"Lord, what a week of tremendous ups and downs... a time of testing that You are allowing, a time of intense spiritual warfare, a time of temptation where I am looking to find some of my need for emotional security and stability in my friendship with Ellen instead of with You! I fear losing this wonderful friendship, so my thoughts have become too preoccupied with her. It's not that I am not to think about her, pray for her, encourage her, or have unfailing "hesed" for her (Hebrew word that means kindness, mercy, steadfast love, compassion). I don't believe the daily emails are a problem; it is part of keeping up a long distance friendship. I do believe You

want me to master this temptation. The enemy is trying to discourage me and entice me to sin, knowing that it can be an area of weakness if I walk according to the flesh. I think it's true I am looking for security and stability at a time of great change in my life, which is not usual for anyone. So, I have struggled with feeling insecure, and the temptation is to find a portion of this security in my relationship with Ellen instead of entirely with You. Oh, Lord, forgive me. I know this kind of security can only be found in You. Lord, help Ellen and me to work through all of this and establish trust in all areas of our wonderful friendship... a friendship that is a gift from You. We both want it to be 100% healthy and pleasing to You!"

I think this excerpt from my journal explains pretty well what was going on, what both of our hearts were in this issue, and how God was using it in my life. God wanted to show me I was healed of emotional dependency, but that does not mean it can never happen again. I'm not to think, "Well, I've arrived; I do not have to worry about ever being dependent on a person when I should be dependent on God." Why? Well, temptations of all kinds will come and go; I just need to watch and pray, staying alert to the lusts of my flesh when they surface and to the wiles of the enemy. But I do trust God, and I know in my heart that without Him I can do nothing. I am dependent on Him, and I trust Him to meet my needs however He sees fit. The result of all of this in my friendship with Ellen was to help us work through some trust issues and to have a better understanding of what we each take into the friendship. I also realized God was not just working in my life, but Ellen's as well. The enemy kept shooting darts of condemnation at my mind: "This is all about you, Ruth; you're screwing up this friendship." In reality, our friendship is good and a gift from God, and stronger for having gone through this trial. Finally, because of ministry, I needed to have clear understanding of God's expectations in relationships and what makes them healthy versus unhealthy. So, in the next chapter we are going to look at God-ordained "relationship rules" He has shown me through His Word.

At this point, please allow me to share one more very recent discovery that has come to the forefront in my life. I now realize my past actions toward my family and extended family did not measure up to my mom's expectations; but my brother's actions did measure up. Thus, in my soul I have felt this deep need for equal acceptance and affirmation in her eyes. This unmet need has played a part in my tendency toward emotional dependency in relationships. As a Christian, I am so grateful to have found my acceptance in Jesus, but still struggle at times with my emotions when not affirmed for something good I have done. But, now because I understand the need behind the emotions, with the Lord's help, I can deal with it properly.

As we wrap up this chapter, I would like you to consider a very important question. Are those leading or coming out of the homosexual lifestyle, especially lesbians, the only ones vulnerable to emotional dependency? No they are not. Anyone, given the right set of circumstances, pressures and opportunities, could end-up emotionally-dependent or in an emotionally-dependent relationship. Remember Ellen's friend who she mentions in her email? As women, God has placed in us the deep need for intimate fellowship and relationship. Though most women may not feel tempted by homosexuality, evidence is strong that we are tempted by dependency. Emotional dependency on another person, male or female, can easily cross the line into a homosexual or an adulterous physical relationship. In the case of Ellen's friend, her dependency lead to a relationship with a woman, ruining both marriages. Even though I cannot take the time to deal with that in this book, please note: it is also unhealthy to become completely dependent on your husband or your children to meet your needs for love and personal security; you should look to God to fill those needs. We need to watch for any temptations in this area and deal with them, for the enemy knows our weak areas and will exploit them. God gives us wonderful relationships for the purpose of meeting various needs and, simply, to bless us! Our lives are about relationships, so let's look at some of God's guidelines for these relationships so they can be the blessing He has intended them to be!

"In learning to build solid friendships we need to **cultivate our ability to find peace and nourishment when we are alone with the Lord and with ourselves.**

"Developing a capacity for solitude involves more than building a strong prayer life or regular time spent reading the Bible. **It involves learning to relax and enjoy God's presence and to enjoy ourselves when we are alone with him.** *We learn to put aside striving and to take in the beauty of everyday life and the world around us. In solitude we cultivate sensitivity and a true appreciation for others.*

"For the **independent person** *solitude provides a place to breathe and regroup before coming back into involvement with others. For the* **person who struggles with emotional dependency**, *time alone offers an opportunity to experience healing and comfort from the Lord directly and to learn appreciation for one's own company. When time alone is welcomed, rather than feared, the anxious drives toward dependency lose much of their power."* [1]

Journal:

March 2007 *"Wow, I can't believe You showed me this... it's totally Your doing, Lord. It was no accident! You are so faithful. It has given us a better understanding of our friendship, and it can be as You designed it! I love you!"*

Chapter 7: Relationship Rules

As we begin this important chapter dealing with God's rules for relationships, I must remind you that after I received Ellen's first email, just as she asked me to, I sought the Lord's view on our relationship. But, it took a good week to sort through everything, because I was also in a battle with my flesh and the devil. I will address the very real warfare that was going on in the next chapter. But, essentially, here's the reality: I needed to make sure the relationship between Ellen and me was God-honoring. It was hard to discern if all aspects of my relationship with Ellen were healthy or not. I was so grateful for a few of the resources that I have already mentioned that give biblical wisdom, so I could prayerfully focus my thinking and ask God for help. But what really helped was the clarification I received through God's Word.

Immediately, I was reminded of a principle from the Bible that I knew to be true. "There is a way that seems right to a man, but its end is the way of death" (Proverbs 14:12). There are two ways of doing things: God's way, which leads to life and blessing; and our way, which inevitably leads to destruction. This principle has a powerful impact in the realm of our relationships. There's our way of pursuing, establishing and maintaining relationships, and then there is God's way. "As for God, His way is perfect" (Psalm 18:30). The contrast between the two is like night and day. Dependent relationships can at first seem so right, but end up being so wrong. Instead of experiencing the safety and the security of a healthy relationship because God is at the center of it, there is the hassle and heartache of a relationship with a destructive end. All my lesbian relationships ended destructively!

God's desire is for our relationships to glorify Him and to bless us. So, let's take a look at God's rules, or principles, for healthy relationships. Remember, we were created relational beings. God, too, is a relational being. Therefore, God is our perfect source for having awesome, God-honoring relationships. This will not be an exhaustive list of God's rules for relationships, but it will include those most important to a person coming out of homosexuality and to those with emotional dependency tendencies.

The first and most important relationship rule, bar none, is Jesus must come first! "I am the vine, you are the branches. He who abides in Me, and I in him, bears much fruit; for without Me you can do nothing" (John 15:5). Our relationship with Jesus must come first because it is through Him that we receive the love, patience, peace, acceptance, understanding, forgiveness, and all other things we need in order to be have right relationships with others. How do we keep our relationship with Him intact and in its rightful place? This question requires a two-part answer.

First, we must keep ourselves from idols! Second, we need to replace any idols that occupy the place in our lives that should be reserved for God with a vibrant relationship with Him. At this point you may be thinking, "Idols? Of course I don't have any idols!" May I remind you of how John ends his epistle of 1 John? "Little, children, keep yourselves from idols. Amen" (1 John 5:21). This short, five-chapter epistle has been referred to as the "Cliffs Notes for Christianity" because it covers all of the essential elements of the Christian life. When John wrote this epistle, he had the benefit of being well-aged and of witnessing the gamut of sins and stumbling blocks that negatively affect believers' lives and relationships with the Lord. When the roots of these sins were traced back, they had a common source: idolatry. It is the sin that nobody thinks they have, yet everybody does have to some degree. John's admonition remains relevant to all of us today.

The warning against idols is also an exhortation to make the Lord our primary pursuit. All that we think, say and do should be screened through this filtering question: How does this impact my relationship with the Lord? Idolatry is something that lurks inside each and every one of us. It does not matter how long you have walked with the Lord. We struggle with it daily, and in most cases, we don't even realize it. It wears a million different masks in our lives: impure passions; shameful desires; an insatiable appetite for more stuff. These are all symptoms of idolatry. The best defense against idolatry is a daily commitment not only to keep ourselves from idols, but also to dedicate our lives to knowing Him better, "seek[ing] first the kingdom of God" (Matthew 6:33).

This first relationship principal is so important. Keep the Lord in first place in your life by keeping yourself from idols! Let's take a look at six more idols specific to relationships and friendships.

- Worry – When I received Ellen's email, I immediately began to worry, "I'm going to lose this friendship." Worry began to overshadow my confidence in God. Was I going to trust Him or was I going to worry about losing this wonderful friendship? I would bow down to God or to worry. Which would it be? I began to pray, "Lord, I'm not going to go there… I'm not going to dwell on the possibility of losing this friendship. Lord, help me! Is there something to be concerned about with our friendship?" When Jesus taught to seek first the kingdom of God, He was offering the perfect prescription for removing the idol of worry: "'Therefore I say to you, do not worry about your life…'" (Matthew 6:25). Several times in the next week, I had to deal with worry and not let it become an idol in my life. No matter what the end result would be of all this soul searching, I willed myself to trust God to work everything out for my good, and for His glory.

- Thoughts and Feelings – I have already talked about the importance of not walking according to our feelings (Chapter 3), and the same was true in this situation. I could let worry and fear that Ellen was going to bail out of the relationship almost paralyze me, or I could trust God and seek His will in it all. Then there was the constant stream of thoughts fueling these feelings. Our thought life can have such a powerful impact on our lives. Would I allow my thoughts and feelings to become an idol and lead me down the path of disobedience? I realized this was a time of trial and temptation, so I needed to take these thoughts captive (2 Corinthians 10:4-5) and set my mind on things above (Colossians 3:2) while I pursued the truth for this situation, the truth that reflects God's thinking, character and will for my situation. At one point, I had to force myself to draw myself close to God in prayer, because I didn't feel like doing it. Would I trust Him or my fleshly thoughts and feelings concerning my friendship with Ellen? Keep in mind, the devil was the source of many of these renegade thoughts, and we will talk about this warfare in the next chapter.

- Relationships – I needed to seek the Lord and ask Him to show me if our relationship had become an idol in my life. Had she become more important to me than the Lord? Here is an important reality concerning relationships: our relationship with a spouse, fiancé, child, parent or friend, has the potential to steal away our hearts from the One who deserves our first love at all times. Whenever this happens, the relationship has over-stepped its rightful place in our lives, and we need to elevate our relationship with God above all else. For example, there were times through the years when I was lonely, and I looked to Ellen to remedy that issue in my life, waiting to hear from her, when I should have first looked to the Lord, drawn close to Him, and elevated my relationship with Him. Then, there were times when I did just that and then shared my feelings with Ellen. God then used her to encourage me to continue to draw close to Him. Or times when after I had elevated my relationship with the Lord, Ellen would bless me with an unexpected call or email and the loneliness dissipated. This is what friends do and yet God was in His rightful place in my heart! This brings me to the next idol.

- Friendships – Friendship is a powerful force. It has the ability to bind people together for a lifetime, which can be good or bad. A friendship that is based on two people who are mutually surrendered to the lordship of Jesus Christ is more valuable than all of the world's riches. However, a friendship that consistently interferes with our relationship with God is a form of spiritual idolatry, or you could call it "friend-ship idolatry." The Bible tells us to choose our friends carefully. "The righteous should choose his friends carefully, for the way of the wicked leads them astray" (Proverbs 12:26). I've talked about the importance of acquiring godly friends for the person coming out of homo-sexuality, but it is important for all believers. Godly friends join us in our desire to please and obey God through words and actions; have a healthy respect for the convictions we have purposed in our hearts; and encourage us to draw closer to our precious Lord. So, we need to take inventory of our friendships, and that's what I did, with the Lord's help. In the case of Ellen and me, our friendship was not an idol that kept either of us from seeking Jesus as we should. In contrast, it has been a friend-ship that encourages and enables us to live for the world to come! "Two are better than one... for if they fall, one will lift up his companion" (Ecclesiastes 4:9-10).

• Lust – The lust of the flesh can easily become an idol, leading us to be disobedient. And when it comes to the morality issues in our life, the lust of the flesh can cause us to please our fleshly lusts instead of pleasing the Lord. We can lust after money, things, or people and put them before God. When our lust for a person becomes an idol, it quite often leads to immorality such as homosexuality, adultery or fornication. Same-sex attraction/feelings originate from the lusts of the flesh. Opposite-sex attraction/feelings for someone God has not given you, such as someone else's husband, are also lusts of the flesh. When we put these things before obedience to the will of God, they become an idol. Now, Ellen was not questioning our relationship because she struggled with any lustful feelings toward me, or had any emotional dependency issues going on in her heart, however, she was not sure what was going on in my heart. This was a trust-issue in our relationship that had to be dealt with. I made it very clear to her that I had never had same-sex attraction/feelings toward her, nor was I emotionally dependent on her.

- Expectations – Our expectations can become idols. The truth is, our greatest disappointments in life are typically attached to our greatest expectations. Sometimes we put expectations on God that we should not, and when He does not deliver as we expect, we are disappointed or offended. These unmet expectations can cause us to turn from God when they are unfilled. We elevate "poor me" above God. Not only do we do this with God, but we do the same thing in our human relationships. In the case of someone who is emotionally dependent on another person, they will resort to manipulation to see that their expectations are met. I was not trying to manipulate our friendship in any way. We did realize, however, that we had some different expectations for friendships;

these expectations were not idols, but they were related to the trust-issues in the relationship. I'll touch on these issues shortly.

So, we must keep the Lord in first place in our lives by keeping ourselves from idols. If you determine something or someone has taken God's rightful place in your life, or is turning you away from your relationship with the Lord and your desire to do His will in your relationships, then elevate your relationship with Jesus and deal with it. Get the Lord back to His rightful place in your life and keep Him the foundation for all other relationships!

Now, let's take a look at several other principles, or good rules, for relationships found in God's Word. And keep in mind, this is not an exhaustive list!

- Allow God's Word to determine what we can and cannot do in our relationships. Otherwise, here's the reality: we will do what is right in our own eyes. We will follow our feelings and the desires of our heart. Here's what the Bible says about our hearts. "The heart is deceitful above all things, and desperately wicked; who can know it?" (Jeremiah 17:9) We need something more reliable than our hearts to lead us in our relationships, and we have it, for God has given us the truth of His Word.
- Learn to be content in all areas of your life, including your relationships. Paul the Apostle said, "Not that I speak in regard to need, for I have learned in whatever state I am, to be

content" (Philippians 4:11). Unfortunately, we often wish for more from the relationships than what God has given us. We wait for something to be added to them when we should be pursuing the contentment that comes from being connected to Christ. The sooner we see our need to dwell in a state of contentment, the sooner we will find contentment in our relationships with others.

- In all close relationships, this is God's will for us: "Do not be unequally yoked together with unbelievers. For what fellowship has righteousness with lawlessness? And what communion has light with darkness?" (2 Corinthians 6:14) I have talked about this principle earlier in the book. The Lord warns us against becoming intimately entangled with those who are unbelievers because He knows this will inevitably lead to spiritual compromise. And our heavenly Father knows best!

- If a relationship has value and worth, then there is an element of cost attached to it. Just think about it. If something has no cost attached to it, what's it really worth? Nothing! Our relationship with Jesus is worth so much because He chose to sacrifice and surrender everything for us. "'Greater love has no one than this, than to lay down one's life for his friends'" (John 15:13). This is an important principle when it comes to our relationship with God, but also, in our other relationships. Life shows us that the relationships worth the most are also the

ones steeped in sacrifice. If we want relationships that are worth something, then we need
to be willing to sacrifice something. We need
to move beyond knowing this, and begin doing
this in the relationships that God has blessed
us with.

- Another important rule for an "active" friendship is that is must be reciprocal. One-way
friendships do not work. "A man who has
friends must himself be friendly" (Proverbs
18:24). If you have a friendship that you neglect
or you communicate very little in, then you
really don't have an "active" friendship. Real
friendships are reciprocal; they require two-
way interaction in order to exist and develop.
They also require effort and investment; they
do not "just happen" on their own. The proverb
mentioned above spells this out by telling us
that if someone wants to have friends, then he
or she must be friendly. It's the age-old principle of reaping and sowing; what we get out
of our relationships really depends on what we
put into them (see Galatians 6:7). All too often,
those persons coming at the friendship from
the dependency side want to rush this principle,
this process. We want the intimacy without the
investment. In essence, we want to reap the
harvest without having to sow the seed. Ellen
and I were working through issues. We were
honestly communicating, and therefore establishing and growing our relationship. We were
investing in it, and that was a good thing! Ask

yourself, how can I do better at sowing into my friendships?

As I prayerfully sorted through what was going on in our relationship, and sought to determine if our friendship was indeed healthy, especially on my part, I found the answer to be "yes," it was healthy. The primary reason was very evident: we both prioritized loving God and keeping our relationship with Him first in our hearts, which is the foundation for all other relationships, including friendships. When God is in His rightful place and you have a vibrant relationship with Him, you can deal with tendencies toward dependency or dependency issues in relationships when you follow His rules. He will enable you, if you will walk by the Spirit. And you know what? It really does work.

Now, before I can share with you one last, very important principle for healthy relationships that the Lord showed us through this process, please go back to the introduction to this chapter and read about "solitude", then bare with me while I set up for you how God ministered to us in a big way through this insightful understanding of solitude. In my first email response to Ellen concerning our relationship, I tried to explain that I had prayed and taken our friendship to the Lord, and I truly believed it was healthy. Here's a portion of her reply with my original thoughts in parenthesis:

"I read your email. I'm glad you feel things are going well. I wanted to make sure that

there's nothing-unhealthy going on in our friendship. So, I guess I won't let it bother me. (It doesn't sound like you are convinced I'm right... hmm!) I've had really close friends before, and haven't felt this way. (What way?) I think I'm just a bit independent as a person. I know with another friend, at times in the past when she'd want to do things with me a lot, and be together all the time, I started feeling a bit suffocated. (Wow, you've been feeling suffocated?) I think these are the dynamics of friendships that people work out. Some people are more independent than others. I think sometimes I feel like if I don't write all the time, I will make you feel bad. And I don't want to make you feel bad. But sometimes I'm busy. (Well, sometimes I am, too. And the amount of time it takes to write all the emails in a week is probably much less than one of the phone calls you get everyday.) So, if I don't email you back right away, every day, don't feel bad, ok?"

Well, I was not convinced that in her heart Ellen really agreed with my conclusion. How did she feel, anyway? So, I prayed, asking the Lord to give me understanding and help me sort through my thoughts and feelings before I emailed her back and asked her to clarify. Here are the key things she said in her reply:

"I want our relationship to be built on trust, that you would know I'm your friend and accept you as you are... that if I don't write everyday it wouldn't be rejection... I want to know I can be me without you feeling hurt, does this make sense? Maybe I'm a little scared... On a personal level, I think we're establishing trust issues... That I can trust that you are okay with me being just who I am, maybe a little more distant emotionally than you. And that you can trust that I'm not mad at you or rejecting you if I don't express myself with love all the time. Intimacy with another female has boundaries for me... and the thought of getting really close is a bit scary for me. And I think you can under-stand my extra uneasiness, because of your history..."

After reading her reply over and over, I asked the Lord to clarify the dynamics of our friendship. He was so faithful to do just that! While Ellen and I are like-minded in many ways, she and I were coming to our relationship from opposite sides of the friendship coin. Therefore, some of our expectations for friend-ship relationships were different. Then, in seeking the Lord and using different resources to focus my thoughts on these specific issues in our relationship, I found an article about solitude and its importance in establishing friendships. When I meditated on her email, I have to admit it hurt a bit that she felt uneas-iness because of my past. I knew without a doubt that my sexual identity as a woman was no longer homosexual, but heterosexual, with all the attractions and feelings that go with it; praise the Lord! And, in all my years as a Christian, I had developed many friendships at different levels of intimacy (from acquaintances to close friends), but none of them had ever shared any feelings of uneasiness due to my past history. I believe that's very unusual, however, and most people coming out of homosexuality will experience an uneasiness in others when building friendships, and especially so for men. Well, very quickly, the Holy Spirit brought to mind these few paragraphs on solitude that I had recently read and pondered. I was blown-away, as I just knew this was it! This small portion of the book explained exactly what was going on and why. I emailed Ellen, telling her I really thought this book excerpt would bless her, because I believed it articulated very well what she was trying to express to me. Here's what she said:

> *"Wow! I just read the attachment. I say amen to that. That is so much how I feel. He says it so clearly. I fall into the independent category, and almost every friend I've been really close to has been the same way."*

This discovery helped both of us immensely! It gave us a much better understanding of each other and what we were each bringing into the relationship. As an independent person, solitude provides Ellen a place to take a deep breath and regroup before coming back into involvement with others. So, if I did not hear from her for awhile, it did not mean she was rejecting me. For the independent person, it is important that they do not remain lone soldiers or in that place of defensive detachment from others. For the person who has struggled with emotional dependency issues, like me, time alone gives me the opportunity to find healing from any insecurities or dependency issues that might arise. This cannot be emphasized enough because time alone with the Lord is the foundation for solid friendships, and the fruit of such time is peace and nourishment. "With solitude of heart as the foundation for relationships comes intimacy in friendship, marriage and community life that is creative." [2] We can strengthen each other by mutual respect and by considering each other's uniqueness and individuality. This keeps us from putting unfair expectations on our friends, allowing them to be themselves. These words about solitude were tremendously insightful and enlightening for both of us to better understand the dynamics of our friendship, and how to better relate to each other in love.

As I am sure you would all agree, we cannot have a growing friendship, or any kind of relation-ship, without encountering some conflicts. It has been said that if two people always agree on every-thing, then one of them is not thinking. Through this experience, Ellen and I have enriched and improved our friendship. What a blessing! I have much more of an understanding of relationships for having gone through this. The things I have learned have not only strengthened my friendship with Ellen, but they have given me much more wisdom in the area of relationships for this ministry. Why so many pages on my friendships with Jill and Ellen? God has taught me so much through them, especially about re-entry into intimate relationships, and the struggles that the person coming out of homosexuality might go through in establishing relationships. Remember, the things I share in this book, are not just unique to me coming out of homosexuality. I pray what I have learned and experienced will help others.

In summary, ex-homosexuals and those struggling with emotional dependency can establish God-honoring relationships. It's a matter of keeping Jesus first in your heart and building all your relationships from that foundation. Build your relationships by following God's rules. He will enable you by His Spirit, so trust Him!

As we conclude this chapter, you need to understand one more thing concerning this week in my life. I had marked out this week as a time to write for this book. It ended up being a time of trial and temptation. By faith, I needed to trust Him to give me overcoming-life to persevere in this time of tribulation (John 16:33). For a day and a half, I thought I had been the victim of identity theft, which caused immediate fear and panic in me that drove me right to Jesus. I got very little sleep. When that got worked out, out of the blue came the first email from Ellen. Working through these relationship issues took several days. I started to feel sick and began to have sinus problems, which I rarely have. There were family concerns that weighed on me and took some of my time. It was a time of extreme spiritual warfare, more things than I can take the time to share. By the end of the week, I was struggling to keep my head above water. I had just enough faith to hang on. I asked for prayer from a group of godly women that I could trust. I have experienced warfare many, many times before, but never this intensely. God was allowing it to prepare me for this ministry. You can expect periods of intense spiritual warfare when you are in ministry. But the truth is, warfare is a reality in the life of every believer. And for the Christian coming out of homosexuality, seeking complete change, you must understand: you will go through spiritual warfare. So, let's take a look at how it might raise its ugly head in your life so you can be ready to do battle God's way! The only way to ensure victory!

Journal:

February 11, 1990: "This weekend spiritual warfare was really going on in my head about Diane. I even dreamt about a relationship with her. Saturday morning I had doubts, thinking I might fall into sin, even though I know it is wrong. I don't want the feelings that have popped up. Please take them away for good!"

Scriptures:

Ephesians 6:10-18a "Finally, my brethren, **be strong in the Lord** and in the power of His might. **Put on** the whole **armor of God,** that you may be able to **stand** against the **wiles of the devil.** For we do not wrestle against flesh and blood, but against principalities, against powers, against the rulers of the darkness of this age, against spiritual hosts of wickedness in the heavenly places. Therefore **take up** the whole armor of God, that you may be able to **withstand** in the evil day, and having done all, to **stand. Stand** therefore, having girded your waist with truth, having put on the breastplate of righteousness, and having shod your feet with the preparation of the gospel of peace; **above all, taking the shield of faith with which you will be able to quench all the fiery darts** of the **wicked one.** And take the helmet of salvation, and the **sword of the Spirit, which is the word of God; praying always with all prayer and supplication in the Spirit.**" (Emphasis mine)

1 Peter 5:6-10 "Therefore humble yourselves under the mighty hand of God, that He may exalt you in due time, casting all your care upon Him, for He cares for you. **Be sober, be vigilant;** because your **adversary the devil** walks about like a roaring lion, **seeking** whom he may devour. **Resist him, steadfast in the faith,** knowing that the same sufferings are experienced by your brotherhood in the world." (Emphasis mine)

Chapter 8: Understanding the Battle

In this chapter we are going to look at the truth concerning spiritual warfare in the life of a Christian. Now, I must ask you this question: when the topic of spiritual warfare is mentioned, what response does it invoke in you? I ask, because many people have a difficult time believing that invisible forces are battling for the sake of us mere mortals. Others live their lives very aware that the physical realm of reality is only one realm of reality and that there is truly more than meets the eye. Yet another group completely dismisses the thought that there is a battle going on between good and evil. Lastly, there are those who see a demon behind every rock. They believe in such things as a "demon of gluttony" that hangs around fast food places and grocery stores; a demon of envy that lives at the Toyota dealership;

and a demon of disease that haunts the local hospitals and medical centers. Well, you get the idea!

So, what camp do you fall in? There is probably *some* degree of truth in all of these perspectives. The Bible clearly speaks about the spiritual war we face. I do believe it is probably bigger and more intense than we can imagine. On the other hand, I also believe we are safer than most Christians believe. In His Word, God lays out for us how to engage in this spiritual battle. We can rest assured that God will fight for us, but to be victorious, we must do our part. Through the Scriptures we will learn, hopefully sooner rather than later, that spiritual warfare is an ever-present reality in the life of a Christian. As you can see from the journal excerpt in the introduction, early in my walk, I knew spiritual warfare was real. To the reader coming out of a homosexual lifestyle and truly seeking complete change in identity and feelings, please understand that this process of change will not be without a battle. So, it was imperative that I learned how the enemy of my soul operates, learned to discern his attacks and understood what my responsibilities are in order to be strong in the battle. You, dear Christian, must do the same! Praise the Lord that we do not have to battle in our own strength, but in the strength of His might!

Let us now take a look at the ABC's of spiritual warfare given to us in God's Word. It would be helpful if you would go back to the introduction of this chapter and read the verses from Ephesians 6 and 1 Peter 5. A good portion of the ABC's will come from these Scriptures. As I identify other

Scriptures that are important to an understanding of the ABC's, and only give you the Scripture reference, I encourage you to look them up in your Bible, especially if they are new to you. Let us now seek to answer the following question: What are the foundational truths we need to know and to put into practice to be victorious in spiritual warfare?

- The enemy of our souls, the devil or Satan, is a deceiver and a liar (John 8:44). There is no truth in him. He is seeking to destroy our walk with the Lord. He has cohorts in the heavenly places helping him in his work.
- God is our defender! We are to be strong in the Lord and in the power of His might, not our own.
- The devil's main style of attack is to deceive. We are to stand against "the wiles of the devil" (Ephesians 6:11). In the original Greek text, the word for "wiles" means "to follow in an orderly and methodical procedure with the intent to deceive." Another rendering of this word is "art form." Satan has made deception into an art form because he knows it is the most effective way to defeat us.
- We are told repeatedly to stand. That is our position for battle, and we do it in the strength of the Lord. Through deception, the enemy draws us away from God and keeps us ineffective Christians in the kingdom of God; we then attempt to operate by fleshly means. So, instead of standing our ground, we sometimes

retreat, or we rail accusations at the devil that we somehow think will chase him away. Yet, God's command is "to stand."

- Put on the armor of God! (Ephesians 6:13-18) This armor is our God-given protection against the attacks of the devil. Satan's attacks often come in ways that are neither obvious nor expected, we must put on our armor everyday. It is to be a way of life for the Christian. We do not have time to study all the parts of the armor now, but I pray you will do so on your own. Because our enemy's main tactic is to shoot the fiery darts of wrong thoughts at our minds, we will concentrate on the shield of faith and the sword of the Spirit (vv. 16-17). These thoughts are knocked down by holding up high the shield of faith to protect our minds. We choose to believe the specific Scriptures the Spirit brings to mind or leads us to the Word that counter these wrong thoughts. Then, no matter what our feelings and circumstances are telling us, we choose to stand on God's truth and promises. When we do that, we are wielding our sword of the Spirit.

- Resist the devil; be steadfast in faith! We might have strongholds in our life that take a while to break down due to the hurts caused by our own past sin or the hurts caused by others. For example, we may struggle with forgiving an abuser in our past, so the enemy will fire away! Or he may fire away with "if only" thoughts of the past. If only I had had a healthy relationship with my mother or father as a child. If only I had not been abused. If we are struggling with our past, then the devil will shoot several different kinds of fiery darts that are disguised as our own thoughts. They could be thoughts of doubt, condemnation, fear and a sense of worthlessness. The cumulative effect of these darts can undermine our faith in God and the truth of God's Word, immobilizing us and drawing us away from the Lord. Thus, it's imperative to have that shield of faith in position. Then we stand on the Word of God and say, "Lord, I know Your Word says You will use everything in my life for my good and for Your glory, and that includes the hurts of my past (Romans 8:28). I also know there is no condemnation for those who are in Christ Jesus (Romans 8:1), and I thank You for that promise."

- We must learn to discipline our thought life. We need to frisk our thoughts at the door of our minds (Philippians 4:8). Are they true thoughts or untrue, unreal thoughts? Are they good thoughts or bad thoughts? Are they pure thoughts or impure thoughts? We must learn to discipline our thought-life so we do not dwell on or meditate on wrong thoughts. We must learn to take every thought captive (2 Corinthians 10:4-6).
- Pray, pray, pray! Humble yourself, and take all your cares to God. Pray continually and persistently, sharing your heart with Him. Ask Him

to show you His will for your situation. God cares, and remember, He wants to help you. He tells you to stand, and He will be strong on your behalf.

- Be sober and vigilant. There is a battle going on for your mind, so we must be diligent to stay alert.

- Remember too, that your flesh can be an enemy all by itself. Our flesh and our spirit have different appetites. The question is, which one are we going to feed? It is imperative, and our responsibility, to walk by the power of the Spirit in us and not according to the lusts or desires of our flesh (Galatians 5:16). If we walk according to our feelings, our circumstances, the world's philosophies, or our vain imaginations (empty thoughts and imaginations that are not true), then the lusts of the flesh can be powerful. But then, throw the devil into the equation, and he will attempt to push all the right buttons to take advantage of our weaknesses. We will find it impossible to resist, to stand and to be victorious in the battle. You must believe and stand on the promises of God specific to your situation, or your sword will remain in the sheath! Our job is to stand, resist and pray. God will deliver us!

Some of you reading this chapter may be thinking, "I am young in the Lord and I do not know many precious promises to choose to believe." First of all, keep in mind, God allows the warfare, and His Word says He will not allow more than we can handle, and He will provide a way of escape (1 Corinthians 10:12-13). I'm sure you know some key truths and promises from the Word that the Spirit will bring to mind, or He will lead you to them. So, draw close to God and ask for His help. He is faithful!

Now, with a better understanding of the battle we will all go through, let's take a look at my week of extreme warfare. The week could be best described as a roller coaster ride caused by a combination of stresses that stirred up a variety of emotions. When I went through the warfare of the first part of the week that I identified in the last chapter (fear of identity theft; family concerns; and the situation with Ellen), I stood firm, holding up my shield of faith, ready to knock down the arrows of fear, doubt, apprehension, anger and so on. Most importantly, I prayerfully stood on the promises of the Word that applied to my situation. Because I had victory in standing firm against the wiles of the enemy, I shared the following thoughts with the Lord in my journal.

"God, thank You for all that's gone on this week, because it all had a purpose. Lord, I desire to be pleasing to You. I ask that Ellen's and my relationship continue to be just what You want it to be, with You at the center. Thank You for the blessing this friendship has been! I need You… be my Rock today and each day. I love You."

I was so grateful for His goodness toward me. I had an inner peace about everything. Now, was the warfare over? The answer is, "No!" There were a few days of silence on Ellen's part, and initially, I felt fine with it. It's just her time of solitude, I thought. But, my peace quickly disappeared. What happened? I did not stay alert in prayer! The attack happened so quickly, it was as though I had been mortally wounded and could not speak, nor did I want to speak, just die! Simply put, I felt so oppressed; I could not will myself to pray.

In Luke 4:1-13, the Bible records for us Jesus' victory against Satan's temptations. May I bring out two specifics about that experience that applied to my situation? One, the devil will look to hit us when we are weak. Jesus' warfare occurred when He was physically weak. In my case, the devil's attack came when I was physically weak (remember, I had not been feeling well), emotionally exhausted and spiritually vulnerable, as there was something God wanted me to deal with that I had not yet done. Two, in Luke 4, we are also told the devil departed watching for the opportune time to strike again. In my situation, the devil's opportune time to strike again was right away, while I was still celebrating the recent victory. I was not holding up my shield of faith high in defense when he bombarded my mind with thoughts that nearly took me out. I was entertaining both true and untrue thoughts, but I could not separate the good from the bad. I needed the Spirit to lead me into the truth, which would then foster my faith.

First, I needed to come to God in prayer, which I was struggling to do. I emailed the women's ministry core team, and told them I barely had enough faith to keep my head above water. Here is a portion of that email:

"I read this morning, 'Experience shows that the most dynamic seasons of spiritual activity are preceded by a season of testing, and if we want to enjoy the one, we must learn to embrace the other.' Even though I know this to be true, I'm struggling to keep my head above water. This morning I told the Lord that I couldn't do this, whatever this is that I'm doing. I don't want to write the book. 'Lord, help,' I cried out to Him, but could pray no further. I'm feeling crushed, broken, perplexed and wanting to give up. Last week, I felt God's staying power through all the warfare and had a peace. I would so appreciate your prayers. By faith, I'm barely hanging on now. I'm definitely not walking by feelings or I'd chuck it all; it's too hard. Thanks for your continued support!"

The women prayed and encouraged me through email to seek the Lord. That morning, I was close to drowning in a sea of the wrong thoughts with which the devil was bombarding my mind and the vain imaginations that I was entertaining. By later that afternoon, the battle had been won, not lost. The next day I recorded in my journal my reflections about the battle.

> *"It was the fear that I really thought I was going to lose the friendship that lead me to sit down and try to pray about this... so I did. I couldn't! I tried to worship with music, and then tried to talk to You, but I knew in my heart that I had not dealt with the insecurity behind it all. I did not trust that You would meet my basic needs for security and love, even though I knew my dependency was in You for all things. Actually, the enemy kept putting in my head the thought that if I trusted You to meet my basic, foundational needs for security and love, then I would lose my friendship with Ellen, a friendship that was such a blessing to me, and why would I want to lose it? There was fear of loss. Even if this friendship dissolved, I knew You would give me wonderful friendships (though inside I was thinking, 'But what about this friendship?'). I finally forced myself to speak to You, and I began to cry, to weep, then to sob! I began to be honest with You and repented of not trusting You. When I surrendered the friendship to You... 'Lord, Your will be done'...everything changed for the good. And I soon realized the fear of loss was a vain imagination!"*

I think you can understand as you read this journal excerpt that I was not hearing God clearly. There was so much clutter in my thinking that I had a hard time hearing, so as to do His will. I was a wounded soldier in battle, and I tried to pray but could not. I asked others to pray, and their prayers of faith saved me and the Lord raised me up (James 5:13-15). Let me explain what was going on and how it all played out.

In our spiritual battles, nothing will take us down faster than sin. In my case, I had been holding on to my friendship with Ellen, however God wanted me to surrender it to Him. From God's perspective, this was the real issue that had to be dealt with. Why is this so important to Him? Jesus tells us if we are going to follow Him, we must surrender to Him our life and everything we have. We find this truth in Luke 18:18-23, when the rich young ruler comes to Jesus and asks Him what he had to do to inherit eternal life. These verses tell us he was a moral young man who kept the Ten Commandments, but he wanted to know what else he had to do. Jesus responds, "'Well, you need to do one more thing. Sell everything, give to the poor and follow Me.'" Jesus' saying was too hard for him; the young ruler could not let go of everything, and thus left sorrowful because he could not follow Jesus.

This is a hard thing that Jesus asks His followers to do, but we must do it. Ponder this: Where does everything good in our lives come from? Our Father in heaven! Jesus knows if we do not surrender all to Him, then we will stay bound to our relationships, homes, comforts, securities, things, attachments of all kinds; they will keep us from doing His will. So, it is wise to pray daily for all aspects of a surrendered heart. Quite likely, we all have things we struggle to let go of for good. If we are going to follow Jesus, then we must surrender all.

Here is another very critical issue concerning this matter. Whenever we refuse to let go of anything or anyone, it will become a target of choice for the devil. He knows it will threaten our peace and eventually keep us from God's will for our lives. This is exactly what was going on in me. I had no peace. The devil's tactics got me focused on myself and enabled him to fuel the fear he had already put in my heart. I was beaten down, and deep down inside, I knew I needed to look to Jesus. I had humbled myself to ask for prayer from others; now I needed to humble myself before God and draw close to Him. I finally forced myself to begin to pray, and I began to cry. I told Him I knew the fear was not from Him, and I repented of not trusting Him. Then I said, "Lord, I give you this friendship… here it is. Your will be done." By submitting to God, I was resisting the devil, and he fled (James 4:7). I was freed to begin to pray earnestly.

The devil's attack had separated me from God. This sudden intense attack with different kinds of fiery darts hitting my mind all at the same time resulted in me tumbling into the way of introspection. This self-consciousness upset my oneness with Christ and produced a wrestling of soul and spirit. My peace was shattered. Oswald Chambers says this concerning self-consciousness, instead of Christ-consciousness:

> "Never allow the dividing up of your life in Christ to remain without facing it. Beware of leakage, of the dividing up of your life by the influence of friends or of circumstances; beware of anything that is going to split up your oneness with Him and make you see yourself separately. Nothing is so important as to keep right spiritually. The great solution is the simple one – 'Come to Me.'" [1]

I was like Jonah; my soul fainted within me, and then I remembered the LORD, and I looked to Him and prayed (Jonah 2:7). When I drew close to my God and put my focus back on Him, He drew close to me (James 4:8). Oh, how quickly things changed! Jesus tells us to come to Him, and He will give us rest (Matthew 11:28). That's what I did, and He fulfilled His promise. He established rest, and I had peace! God is faithful and so good!

When I had finished praying, I moved into my wonderful sunroom and began to work on chapter 5 of this book. I worked until I realized it was dark outside, and I had not eaten all day. It was amazing! I knew a final healing had taken place.

Yes, the enemy had been tempting me, sifting me like wheat and seeking to destroy me. In Luke 22:32, Jesus told Peter that the devil wanted to sift him like wheat, but He had prayed Peter's faith would not fail. In the end, I realized my faith had not failed. I stood and truly benefited from my armor, especially my shield of faith. Praise the Lord that my faith continues to grow as a result of these times of trial and temptation.

While I was hard-pressed on every side by troubles, perplexed, and knocked down, when I finally got honest with God and repented of not trusting Him and surrendered the friendship, I realized I was not crushed or forsaken, and the friendship was not taken away or destroyed and me with it (2 Corinthians 4:8-9). The wiles of the enemy had been at work to keep me from surrendering the friendship to Jesus. God wanted me to surrender it into His hands, so it would not get in the way of following Him or doing His will for my life. God had this very important purpose in allowing this time of testing in my life!

But I also received some "spoils from the battle." My friendship with Ellen was actually strengthened and more firmly established. I knew without a shadow of a doubt that our friendship was good and God-glorifying, a wonderful gift from God. I knew God had done a work in me that was necessary to prepare me for Bridge of Hope Ministry. Also, this intense week of warfare became book material indeed! Last, but not least, having gone through this warfare, I know my God in a deeper way. Of this I have no doubt: all He did that week was for my good and for His glory!

As we wind down this chapter, I exhort you with all of my heart not to be ignorant of the wiles of the enemy nor of the power of your flesh. When the battle begins, humbly submit to God, placing your all on the altar. Stand strong in the Lord and in the strength of His might, and the devil will flee. Throughout your walk with Jesus, continue to be transformed by the renewing of your mind, so you will know that acceptable, good and perfect will of God for your life and for your circumstances, which includes your times of spiritual warfare. In this obedience is your victory. Stand firm and resist by faith through prayer, trusting in the promises of God and then watching the deliverance of the Lord. Then, just as I received the spoils of my victorious battle, you too will receive the spoils of your victorious battle. Remember, while the devil means every temptation and battle for evil in our lives, God allows them for good in our lives. Knowledge of the truth concerning God's perfect will for your life does not assure you spiritual stability or your victory, but applying the truth to your life does! What we know about spiritual warfare is really useless unless it is linked to our daily lives through practical participation. In Matthew 7:24-26 Jesus tells us:

> "'Therefore whoever hears these sayings of Mine, and does them, I will liken him to a wise man who built his house on the rock... Now everyone who hears these sayings of Mine, and does not do them, will be like a foolish man who built his house on the sand.'"

It is important to understand the battle so that we can do battle! When the enemy attacks, or your flesh rears up, you can have victory! Be wise and not fools, using the weapons of warfare God has given us. When you do, you can know that God will fight for you. God has given us everything we need for life and godliness (2 Peter 1:3), so press on, my friend; press on!

Journal:

October 15, 2005: *"Oh, Father, giving my announcement today at church about BOHM was an emotional and a blessed time. I was so overwhelmed by what You have done in my life... after the service I received so much input and encouragement that this ministry is needed, and I even had opportunities to minister to some people who have family or friends who are homosexual. So many people were eager to give ministry cards to family members and people they worked with. I had talks with so many people I don't even know! Father, I'm blown away... You truly do use the foolish things (and people) of the world to confound the wise. Father, use this ministry in a mighty way to accomplish Your purposes! Bring many into the kingdom; help those coming out of homosexuality to grow in You; and Lord, I especially pray that Your church would minister in love to both these groups of people. Lord, I pray BOHM can be a huge help to the church."*

Chapter 9: Someone I Love Is Gay

At this juncture in the book, it is necessary for me to switch gears and speak to my brothers and my sisters in Christ. Most likely, if you are reading this book and not struggling in the area of homosexuality, then someone you know and love says they are homosexual, not heterosexual. They may be a spouse, a family member, a friend, a neighbor or a co-worker. Through many conversations with people in the church, I have discovered many believers are not sure how to respond to the homosexual; they have many questions. It is my prayer that the previous chapters in this book, including my testimony and all the things I learned after coming out of the homosexual lifestyle, have helped you to gain an understanding of the homosexual and of the lifestyle. I hope you have acquired many Biblically-based insights to help you minister to those caught up in the lifestyle or those struggling with same-sex attractions. And most importantly, I pray you now believe the very real truth that in Christ, anyone seeking to come out of homosexuality can be successful and can change completely. So, when God puts someone in your life who is gay, it is my hope that you will be there for that person, to encourage and to compassionately help him or her work through their struggles! I also pray you desire to help the Christian who is struggling with the unwanted, but very real same-sex attractions and feelings. Here is a very important reality. Both groups are a huge mission field where the laborers are few. But, why would that be? As I have studied the situation, this is what I have found to be true.

There are two philosophies prevalent in society. The first you know already, as I have spoken of it throughout the book: many people believe homosexuality is a genetic situation, that a person is born homosexual. It is purely physical in nature and cannot be changed. Any attempt to change the homosexual will result in denial of true sexual feelings and create additional psychological problems for the individual. Black is black; white is white. There can be no real change. Those people involved in homosexuality are not aware of, or refuse to acknowledge, information from secular studies that show the homosexual is not born that way. [1] Also, many people in the church have touted the second prevalent philosophy: homosexuality is purely a deviant and perverted behavior chosen by the individual. It persists because the individual refuses to repent and offer himself or herself completely to God. Those who have never been tempted in this area often hold to a narrow, often uncompassionate, view that the sin scores a 10 on a scale of 1-10, and that it is **entirely** willful and premeditated. Still others in the church negatively embrace both sides of the issue by condemning and assuming that there can be no change.

As a result of these conflicting philosophies within our churches, the Christian struggler (yes, Christian struggler) is most often silently over-whelmed in the controversy. He or she feels the guilt, shame and loneliness, but also knows that there was never a conscious choice to have or develop homo-sexual attractions. Much of secular society sends a clear message: You cannot and do not need to change, while many in the church agree, ignore or condemn, not understanding that the attractions and feelings developed. The struggler is thereby trapped inside walls of fear and isolation.

Remember, homosexual behavior is sin. Homosexual feelings are not. If the feelings persist, further confusing and leading the individual into the homosexual behavior, the hole of despair, guilt and loneliness deepens until it becomes a trap; a pit which, seemingly, even with God's help, cannot be escaped. There appears to be no way out... no way to break the lust-repentance cycle... no way to live a victo-rious life for the Lord... thus, no hope! Praise the Lord, many like me have found out there is hope!

God has provided a way for escape. With adequate help and counsel by those like you, dear reader, who now clearly understand the problem and the fact that the attractions developed, the struggler can understand the truth that they can truly change. With the help of knowledgeable and compassionate believers, they begin to see clearly the issues behind the development of these attractions. Then one-by-one, they can be taken to the cross for healing. The individual begins to see himself or herself as the person God created them to be. The walls of fear and isolation come down. They can begin to develop healthy, positive, and intimate relationships because they are free from the bondage of homosexuality (feelings and behavior). The first step toward freedom from bondage to same-sex attractions and from bondage to the homosexual lifestyle is to be born again. This means someone must care enough to invest in their life and share the gospel, as Jill did with me.

But, I must present to you another problem that keeps believers from investing in this mission field. As our society more and more embraces homosexuality, this acceptance stirs up a boiling pot of emotions in Christians, especially **fear**. We turn on the television, read a newspaper or go on the Internet and are confronted with homosexual issues, gay-marriage, gay rights and AIDS. More and more television programs and movies glorify the lifestyle and the K-12 public schools and the universities promote it as a healthful, alternative lifestyle. As a result of society's acceptance, many mainline Protestant denominations continue to abandon the literal, Biblical view of homosexuality. More recently, there are many evangelical Christians who now say they do not know what to believe about homosexuality. One leading evangelical pastor, for instance, recently said this: "Most of the emerging leaders I know share my agony over this question… Frankly, many of us don't know what we should think about homosexuality." [2] As a result of all these things, many Christians are **confused** and do not know what to think. When you think of homosexuality, do images of parading, militant homosexuals shouting for rights come to mind? Or perhaps you think of stereotypes: effeminate, flamboyant men and tough women. The thoughts are repulsive to most. Fear is normal, and the well-fortified walls of defense that go up seem to be appropriate. These walls seem necessary to aid you in the protection of your families and the containment of such "aberrations." But, when it hits close to home, and you are faced with a gay or lesbian spouse or family member, or friend or coworker or boss, you struggle between accepting them and **rejecting** them **as people.**

We end up with a war going on all around us. On one side of the wall we have the church, which for the most part, has chosen to either ignore or severely criticize the homosexual as well as the sin. Many believe it is a problem "out there somewhere," but not within the sanctuary. Nothing could be further from the truth. Then, on the other side of the wall is the homosexual who screams to the true, Bible-believing Christian, "You are unloving and homophobic," when we say homosexuality is sin. "You are fanatical and brainwashed because your attitudes have been affected by anti-gay bigotry and intolerance from your families, pastors and churches, who have preached to you and pounded in your head that homosexuality is wrong." And then there is a third party involved here, a party who has a vested interest in this battle; it is the devil. He is right there seeking to deceive both sides. His deception causes the struggler to give up in despair and those who could be, and should be, ministering to the homosexual to react in fear, in hate and without compassion. It is time, dear brother and sister, to claim the unfailing power of God. Speak the truth in love. Remember, Jesus spoke in defense of the woman caught in adultery by looking at her accusers and quietly saying, "'Let he who is without sin cast the first stone'" (John 8:7). They walked away in shame. The woman had sinned and was responsible for her actions, but she received complete compassion from our Lord. The accusers were, technically, correct in their accusation, nevertheless, Jesus rebuked their critical hearts.

It is true homosexuals have their own sub-culture, and there is a minority trying to force acceptance of gay rights and gay marriage. You may even support or be an active member of a Christian group standing up for family values, and that is important. But when we hear such a blatant, and often obnoxious, assault on family values and other morality issues, it irritates our flesh; I am no different from you on this matter. However, we cannot let that affect our relationship with those people the Lord brings into our path who He wants us to establish a relationship with and minister to. When we let this minority get to us, we will act in an unloving manner and more importantly, we will not glorify Jesus in all we say and do. No matter what they say to us or what labels they ascribe to us, such as unloving, homophobic, or bigot (and they can get nasty), we should not act as they act. Here's what Jesus tells us in Matthew 5:44-45: "'But I say to you, love your enemies, bless those who curse you, do good to those who hate you, and pray for those who spitefully use you and persecute you, that you may be sons of your Father in heaven.'"

As followers of Jesus, we must not sit in our pews ignoring, judging or fearing neither the unsaved homosexual nor the wounded brother or sister in Christ. Please, please allow me help you by giving you the two main goals you should be hoping and praying for in the life of the person who you know and love and is gay. The immediate goal is that they accept Jesus as their Lord and Savior, and then seek to come out of homosexuality because it is God's will for their life. The succeeding goal is that complete change takes place in their life. Through the reading of this book, you have found truth that can help you minister the love of Jesus. It's my prayer that any critical hearts have been replaced with hearts of compassion, and that therefore, you have the desire to do just that: minister the love of Jesus to a hurting soul!

If God has put a homosexual in your path or a struggler with same-sex attraction feelings, **how do you invest in their life** so as to have an opportunity to minister to them? Remember, it's God who will save the person, but He wants to use you!

- **Pray, pray, pray**! Pray for yourself that you have God's heart for the unsaved. Pray and ask God to increase your love for the person He has put in your life. The homosexual is deceived and needs Jesus! Pray for their salvation just as you pray for others in your life who do not know Jesus personally! Ask the Lord to open a door of communication with them. Ask Him to break down any walls that may keep you from having a relationship with them. Ask for wisdom.

- **Develop a relationship with this person, if possible**. The most effective evangelism really requires relationship. A recent survey reveals that the majority of those polled were won to Christ while conversing with a friend; through a church service; through their upbringing in a Christian home; or while conversing with family. Jesus is our example for personal evangelism. As we learn in John 4, He took a cynical Samaritan woman of low morals and changed her into a devoted worshiper of God. It is a real glory story, but it was only possible because Jesus first initiated a relationship with her by simply asking her for a drink of water.

- **Be a listener**. This shows that you care and you are not just preaching to them. They may bring up God in conversation!

- **Ask questions** to see how they went down this path. Their answers will give you further wisdom.

- **Share your faith in Christ, and thus the gospel, as the Lord leads**. Share your testimony, and be vulnerable about your own personal struggles and temptations. Remember, your goal is to lead them to Jesus, not to change them. We cannot do that anyway, but we can lead them to the One who can change them.

- **Instill hope for change** (1 Corinthians 6:11). Remember, Paul said, "And such were some of you." Thousands of men and women have overcome homosexuality. They can be completely heterosexual in time, and not just leading a celibate life while still struggling with same-sex attractions forever. Educate yourself about the availability of other books where they can read about other men and women who have come out of homosexuality and have completely changed. If they seem to be open, then ask them to read my book or one of the others.

- **Respond in love**. Speak the truth in love, but remember it's not about cramming Scriptures down their throat or continually beating them over the head with the fact that homosexuality is sin and an abomination, or coming across in any self-righteous way that you would never sin like that, just as the self-righteous religious leaders of Jesus' day claimed. We are to be a reflection of Jesus. Remember the woman caught in adultery in John 8? Jesus did not condemn, He told her to go and to sin no more. Neither should we condemn the homosexual.

- **Communicate to them acceptance** for themselves as a person. Remember, that's what Jill did with me. She did not reject me. She could have said, "Okay, the friendship goes no further, and I'm out of here!" Instead, she communicated her love and acceptance for me, but did not condone the lifestyle. "God loves you and so do I, but I believe homosexuality is wrong, and you need to deal with that with God." Many homosexuals are plagued with rejection deep down inside, and additionally, they often feel further rejection from the Christian community, whether it is real or unreal. After I was saved, I read Romans 8:1, and it so ministered to me because of the rejection I felt inside. "There is therefore now, no condemnation for those who are in Christ Jesus." This verse freed me from those deep feelings of rejection.
- **Affirm love** for the person and **commit** to the person, especially, through prayer. Remember, they are lost and need Jesus.
- **Pray more!** Remember, the effectual, fervent prayer of a righteous person avails much (James 5:16). And get others to pray!

Investing in the life of these individuals does not mean you must become best friends with them or spend all of your time with them. Not so! You invest in their life with the love of Jesus that is flowing in you and through you to them. You make prayer your number one priority. If you seek to invest in their lives as I have outlined above, they will see Jesus in you, and that will make a difference. God will have an opportunity to use you.

At this point, may I specifically address you parents, when that someone you know and love who is gay is your son or your daughter? Having a son or daughter "come out" and be openly gay is usually a shocking discovery, to say the least, and almost always immediately puts you in extreme emotional turmoil. And my heart truly goes out to you. Some immediately feel intense pain and failure as a parent. Some experience extreme panic, as they think, "What will I tell my friend, my church, etc.?" Some feel overwhelming guilt as they blame themselves.

When you are confronted with a child who tells you they are gay, how should you respond? A good way to respond is the following: "I don't understand, and you know God says it's wrong, but I love you and God loves you, and we'll work things out." In this way, you continue to affirm God's love **and your love** for them, while working out **this new relationship** with your son or daughter. They will continue to think you are wrong not to condone their lifestyle, but as Christians, you cannot. As you accept them as a person, they should also accept you, in spite of your beliefs that homosexuality is wrong. And yet, when you do not accept the lifestyle, your son or daughter may stay out of your life, especially if they cannot dictate the rules for your new relationship with them. This is only because deep down inside, he or she knows you are right, and they do not want to deal with the continual conviction and conflict. They just want to "be happy" and "do their own thing!"

After the initial response to their coming out and your finding out, your emotions may take over. With God's help you must work your way through this emotional turmoil. It is really a grief cycle you will quite likely experience because you have lost your child as you know and love them. This is now a different person. Suddenly, you may feel like you are talking to a stranger. Life may seem out of control. You may begin to think about loss of your reputation, but at the core of these emotions spinning out of control is the loss of relationship with your child!

You will find it necessary to work through the shock with its accompanying emotions and physical symptoms such as nausea, migraines, sleeplessness, etc. Some parents enter into denial that there is a problem. Then you may cycle into a phase of protesting through anger, and then enter into a phase of wanting to isolate from others, and you resist getting back to normal where you would have to deal with the situation. I tell you all this so you do not think you are going crazy. And parents, it is so important that you remember you are in this together! So, what are the most important things you as a parent can do to deal with this emotional turmoil?

- **Pray!** Cry out to God! As we often read in the Psalms, "Oh Lord, I need you to be my refuge and my strength, my very present help in this time of trouble. Oh, Lord, how this hurts." You need to will yourself to focus on God as your flesh will want to rule, and your emotions will be all over the place. Ask for God's heart for your son or your daughter. Work through your anger issues with God, which will enable you to be in that place where you can affirm your love for your child. Remember that the love in you is God's unconditional love that is not dependent on your child's actions, and ask God to help you commit to your relationship with your child, just as our Father in heaven stays committed to us. Pray for strength to endure all the emotional conflicts and to be open to ask your child for forgiveness if the Lord shows you something you did that was wrong in your relationship with your child!

- **Get wisdom** for your relationship with your child and, as much as it is up to you, endeavor to restore the relationship if it is broken. The Bible tells us that God's wisdom is always available to every believer; "If any of you lacks wisdom, let him ask of God, who gives to all liberally and without reproach, and it will be given to Him" (James 1:5). Pray for wisdom for the decisions you must make in order to establish rules for when your child desires to come home with his/her lover. Do not deny the truth of God's Word in your decision-making even though your child might not like it. For example, do not condone immorality in your house by allowing them to sleep together. It is so important that you plan ahead and know what your expectations are for behavior when he or she comes home. Here is another reality! Some who minister and counsel in this area will encourage you to say they cannot even come home. Others will say the child can come home, but not with their partner. Others will say they can come home together, but cannot sleep together, desiring to minister to both of them. There are some gray areas here which you as parents have to pray about together, agree upon and then hold to. This is what is important to keep in mind. You are the parents, and the child should not dictate to you in your home. Those living the homosexual lifestyle are often very controlling. They may threaten to never see you again if you do not do such and such. Do not succumb to their pressure-tactics for fear of losing your child. According to God's Word, children are to honor their parents, even if they are of age. In your home they are to be obedient to your rules. Parents, remember you are in this together, so continue to communicate with each other and pray together so you do not react differently when you encounter any confrontational attitudes with your child. Here is the hardest reality for many parents: some children will follow through on their threat to take off and not come home, severing their relationship with you. They continue in the lifestyle with no immediate desire to get right with the Lord! Pray for their salvation if they do not have a personal relationship with Jesus. If they have walked away from the Lord, then pray for the conviction of the Holy Spirit to lead them to repentance. You have to be able to "let go." Surrender and commit your relationship with your child into God's very capable hands. Pray, "Lord your will be done in my child's life." Remember, no one loves your son or daughter more than your compassionate Father in heaven.

- **Get others to hold you up in prayer.** You must continue to seek the Lord's will for all aspects of this situation. Never stop praying for your son or daughter! Don't give up! Prayer is powerful!

So, whether you are the spouse, parent, friend, sibling, or coworker of the homosexual God has placed in your life, in order to minister to them, you must seek to establish and to maintain a relationship; respond in love and pray, pray, pray! Once the person you know and love is saved, the next goal for their life is for complete change to take place as they desire to please God and glorify Him with their life. **How do you continue to invest in their life?**

- Pray, pray, pray! Pray for the person desiring change to walk by faith and not by feelings. Pray for wisdom in ministering to them. Pray for them to be kept from the wiles of the enemy, as warfare will be a reality. Pray that they hold up to the pressures and pull of the old life. Pray until they are strengthened and grow in their walk with Jesus.

- Be a godly role model. If you are of the opposite sex, try to connect them with someone of the same-sex who can help them learn how a godly, heterosexual man or woman should act.
- Love them continually with the love of Jesus.
- Speak the truth when needed. For example, if they want to continue to live with their same-sex partner, then tell them God's will for them is to come out from among them, and be separate and to flee immorality!
- Give them hope that they can change… "and such were some of you."
- Encourage them to get into Bible study. If you have the opportunity, do a Bible study with them.
- Help them find a Bible-teaching church if they are not attending one.
- Encourage them to find Christian fellowship and develop Christian friendships.
- Help them find Biblically-based resources to help them understand how same-sex attractions and feelings took time to develop in their life and how it will take time for them to go away.
- Encourage them that God will complete the work in them that He has started.
- Pray some more!

There **is hope** for the one coming out of homosexuality and for that person struggling with same-sex feelings. First they need Jesus and then a heart to seek change. They also need brothers and sisters in Christ to invest in their life.

We must also keep in mind that there are believers, men and women of all ages, who are sitting in our churches struggling with same-sex attractions and feelings. Yes, this is reality, and no one knows they are struggling. When they were saved, their unwanted attractions and feelings did not automatically go away. As I alluded to in the beginning of this chapter, they are silently overwhelmed and trapped in the controversy concerning homosexuality. They **do not understand why they have these unwanted attractions and feelings**, that is, the things I explained in chapter 4. They perceive they have a sexual problem. They do not understand that their sexuality is an outward manifestation of an inward brokenness that happened when they were a child. They sit in silence for fear of rejection. Many will eventually give up and leave the church and make the decision to enter the mainstream of the homosexual lifestyle where they will find acceptance and affirmation. As one thinks about the people struggling in our churches, the real tragedy is the spouse who comes forward and says, "I cannot struggle with these feelings and fantasies any longer." They have tried to have a healthy, intimate, stable relationship with their spouse, and may have children, only to feel lonely and depressed because of these unwanted feelings that no one knows about. Finally, they tell their spouse their struggle, and now there is the potential for a broken family.

Please let me address the issue of finding out your mate has been living a double life. Your life and your home, so stable the day before, now seem to be collapsing all around you. The discovery leaves emotional devastation everywhere. How can you go on? What should you do?

Well, you must find support for yourself. First of all, cry out to God. But, quite likely, you will need support and input from others. You may seek advice and get conflicting advice. One person may counsel you to leave if your spouse has committed adultery and could give you AIDS. Another person may sternly advise that you stay in your marriage because God will honor your submissive obedience. Here is wise counsel concerning whom to seek for proper support from Anita Worthen's book, <u>Someone I Love Is Gay</u>.

1) Look for input from people who are supportive of your marriage. The Bible is blunt: God hates divorce (Malachi 2:16). Those who give quick advice to break up a marriage are not encouraging you to consider God's perspective on this subject, nor are they being sensitive to the deep commitment which you may have toward your marriage.

2) Look for input from people who have known both you and your spouse over a long time period. Their perspective on the situation and the relationship may be the more balanced than the perspective of a person who has only known one or both of you for a short time period.

3) Look for input from people who understand the root cause and healing of homosexuality.

A homosexual problem does not necessitate divorce. Many spouses who have wrestled with this issue have maintained their marriage; some even now minister to others caught in the same predicament. The issue of when and if to pursue divorce is a decision that should be considered only after thorough discussion with others who can give you godly direction, such as your pastor or other spiritual mentors who can give realistic, yet biblical, counsel. Whatever decision is made, you will need lots of emotional support as you move ahead with your life.[3]

The issues of separation and divorce are highly emotional topics in evangelical churches today. Because an increasing number of Christians have divorced, the way churches deal with this situation has been affected. To stay balanced on this issue, it is important to remember that although God hates divorce, Jesus allowed for it in cases of sexual unfaithfulness (Matthew 19:9). As a spouse dealing with this issue, I would encourage you to get Anita's book or to seek other resources with a biblical view on the issue, but let me offer some guidance to you if you are committed to your marriage and your spouse appears to be making efforts to overcome homosexuality.

- Pray, pray, pray! Pray for strength to endure, especially right after discovery. Bathe the situation in prayer. Warfare will be a reality. Pray for your spouse to see the underlying emotional needs that are behind the homosexuality. Pray that your spouse will see the destructive impact this has on your life and your children's lives. Pray for God's will for your situation. Pray for God's heart for your spouse.

- Give verbal encouragement by telling your spouse you are praying for him or her.
- Keep your own spiritual walk with Jesus in order.
- Keep your own interests, hobbies and relationships during this period in your life. Homosexuality should not become the main theme of your existence, even though it may be a major focus for your spouse right now.
- Do not become a parent to your spouse. Do not nag or try to be your spouse's main source of accountability now.
- Be willing to work on your marriage issues as well.
- Have your own accountability group.

These points will help to keep you in that place where God can minister His will for your life and you will also have the support you need.

As we conclude this chapter, please allow me to share my heart with you, dear brothers and sisters in Christ. You can make a difference in this huge mission field all around us, and I believe God wants to use you. You have taken the time to read this book and gain knowledge and understanding of the lifestyle and how you can help the people caught up in the lifestyle. Therefore, it is my hope and prayer that more and more, the true church of Jesus Christ will be a place strugglers and those desiring to come out of homosexuality will find the love of Jesus and not the condemnation of the devil; the truth about the lifestyle they need to hear, but not jokes about the lifestyle or put-downs about homosexuals that I heard in my church. It only momentarily irritated me, but others are more sensitive. It is hard to come across as loving when you are participating in these kinds of actions. And even if you really are loving and those comments are only sad attempts at humor, you will be perceived as unloving. May the church and believers in general also be people with compassion for those caught up in or affected by homosexuality. Lastly, I hope and pray those seeking change find in the church the all-important Christian fellowship they need. It is that Christian fellowship that is cited by many ex-homosexuals as the most important relational factor that helped them successfully work through the process of change.

In closing, remember, the homosexual is deceived and needs the love of Jesus that can change their life. As you invest in the life of that homosexual God brought into your life, remember the importance of loving the sinner and hating the sin. Resist the temptation to hate because of the actions of an activist minority, yet still stand firm against what is sin; God's love is able to come through that obedient, neutral zone between the two extremes. May you be that conduit in your one-on-one relationship where God's love can flow through you to that someone you know and love who is gay. In so doing, of this you can be sure: your Father in heaven will be greatly pleased, and you will glorify Him.

BRIDGE OF HOPE MINISTRY WEBSITE

www.bridgeofhopeministry.org

The purpose of the website is to:

- Bring **hope** that those struggling can be healed.
- Encourage and present **truth** through my testimony, my personal journal entries, Bible studies, Q & A, and resources that can be a catalyst for true change to take place in the homosexual.
- Give **honest, biblical** advice through email.
- Provide others with the **knowledge** and **understanding** of the lifestyle and the Scriptural **guidance** necessary to minister God's **love** to the homosexual.

EMAIL COMMENTS

- "Thank you, thank you, this ministry is so needed… I've got friends to direct to this website." A sister in Christ
- "I lived as a homosexual 25 years… I so appreciate your website! I read your testimony; much was like a reflection of my life! The Bible studies are what God has shown me!" Steph
- "Wanted to encourage you! I spent time on your website pondering your testimony and what God has taught you. The next day I ministered to a practicing lesbian." Erik

- "Fantastic! I loved your testimony... a pastor found out a person in ministry is a practicing homosexual... I forwarded your page with the resources."
- "There is a woman in my fellowship I would like to direct to your website." Pastor
- "Praying for the ministry! Maybe you can share with our group." Sandy

Chapter 10: Ministry of Truth and Hope

Here we are in the last chapter of the book, and our time together is nearing an end. In the previous pages, you have had the opportunity to gain an understanding of the homosexual and the lifestyle through my testimony and the things that I have learned through my personal change-process. Dear reader, do you now understand and truly believe that real change is possible for the person seeking to come out of homosexuality? Dear brothers and sisters in Christ, do you now understand the important role you play in the life of that one you know who is homosexual, whether they are seeking change or not? It is my prayer that your answers are a resounding, "Yes!" Before I conclude the message of this book, I would be remiss if I did not do one more thing, that is to warn you about the gay agenda and the pro-homosexual theology which are both propagating deceptive myths about homosexuality that society is buying into hook, line and sinker. I fear, "lest somehow, as the serpent deceived Eve by his craftiness, so your minds may be corrupted from the simplicity that is in Christ" (2 Corinthians 11:3). So as to not be deceived, please allow me a few moments of your time to draw your attention to two of the lies peddled as truth. While the majority of same-sex strugglers are not activists, they may defend the lifestyle from these two perspectives. I cannot take the time to go into this in depth, but you can do your homework and see if there are truly facts to back up my statements (and there are). I will make sure to note two good resources for you to reference.

The first myth being touted as truth, most notably through the public schools, is this: homosexuality is a healthy alternative lifestyle. Homosexual activists attempt to portray their lifestyle as normal and healthy and insist that homosexual relationships are in every way equivalent to heterosexual relationships. These relationships are portrayed as loving and committed relationships by Hollywood and the media, who relentlessly propagate the image of the fit, healthy, and well-adjusted homosexual. The reality is quite the opposite. Gay and lesbian relationships are typically characterized by instability, promiscuity, and unhealthy and risky sex practices, factors which greatly increase the incidence of serious and incurable sexually transmitted diseases (STDs), including hepatitis, HPV, syphilis, gonorrhea, and AIDS. [1]

This lie really grieves my heart, as my brother died of AIDS in 1993. About that time, there was a huge push to educate gays to wear condoms, to get tested for HIV and to be responsible to disclose to their sexual partners that they are HIV-infected. At that time, the media was the most important tool used to help educate all of society concerning these HIV/ AIDS issues. Have you noticed, however, there is no longer mention of HIV and AIDS as it relates to same-sex practices? There is no media attention given to this issue. We only hear about the terrible epidemic of AIDS in children in Africa or other places. Why? Is it no longer an issue to be feared and dealt with by the homosexual? No, it is just as much a threat to the life of a promiscuous gay as ever before. While medications help with the symptoms and side effects of the virus and may prolong the life of one infected, they will quite likely live with many health problems before the disease finally takes their life. And do not think for one minute that the lesbian lifestyle is healthy. The majority of lesbians struggle with depression and dependencies of all kinds, including emotional, alcohol, drugs, and food. Oh, and one last very important fact: the suicide rate is much higher for the homosexual than for the heterosexual. Well, this is enough so that you get the idea; the homosexual lifestyle is anything but healthy. My heart breaks for those people so deceived in their thinking that they actually believe homosexuality is a healthy, alternative lifestyle. How has this myth spread and become widely accepted as truth?

It is all part of the strategy of the gay agenda to market homosexuality as a normal and healthy lifestyle. [2] And if anyone cries out against the promotion of homosexual agenda, then they are immediately labeled an unloving, homophobic and a bigot by the media which then turns around and promotes sympathy for the "persecuted" homosexual. At the core of the gay agenda is a huge publicity campaign to affirm homosexuality and win them special rights. Whether it is at the heart of a religious scandal, political corruption, radical legislation or redefinition of marriage, homosexual interests have come to characterize America. How did this happen? It was helped along and promoted by an ever-increasing glut of television shows and Hollywood movies portraying the happy, healthy, loving and well-adjusted homosexual.

The question must be asked: "How should you respond to the success of the gay agenda? Should you accept the recent trend toward tolerance, or should you side with those who exclude the homosexual, and decry the sin?" The Bible calls for a balance between what some people think are two opposing reactions – condemnation and compassion. The truth is that they are both essential elements of Biblical love, and that is something the homosexual desperately needs. As you interact with homosexuals and their sympathizers, you must affirm what the Bible says about homosexuality; it is sin. This is not unloving. You are not trying to bring damnation on those caught up in this lifestyle. You are trying to bring conviction so that they turn from sin and embrace the only hope of salvation for all sinners which comes through faith in the Lord Jesus Christ. Homosexuals need salvation and forgiveness! Therefore, we must speak the truth in love, and then lovingly accept and assist in any effort of those who desire to overcome this sinful lifestyle.

If you have the opportunity to interact with homosexual advocates, you will quite likely be hit with another myth foundational to the gay agenda. It is the myth touted as truth through the gay theology, that homosexuality is part of God's design for men and women. [3] Through the gay theology, the gay agenda successfully sells their warped interpretations of passages in Scripture that address homosexuality. When you ask a homosexual what the Bible says about homosexuality, they will give you an interpretation that is distorted and irrational. This gay theology is being disseminated by those individuals leading and attending both gay churches and churches who do not interpret the Scriptures literally. Thus, this wrong theology is affecting many churches and real Christians so that they are now accepting homosexuality as normal and God-approved.

Dear Christian, let me just be blunt here. What does your Bible really say about homosexuality? We studied those portions of Scripture within the pages of this book. When you interpret His Word literally, as you should, God is clear on the issue. Simply put, the Bible says what it says and means what it means. Your interpretation is only cloudy when the Scriptures are twisted and taken out of context. Do you believe this pro-gay theology that is influencing the homosexual so that they remain in bondage to this sinful lifestyle and do not come to a true and saving relationship with Jesus Christ? This is a great travesty! Oh, church, please be ready to speak the truth to that one you who know and love and is gay. Dear struggler, if these words of mine pierce your soul and make you angry, I understand. Remember, I bought into the lie I was born a lesbian. But consider this: what if my Biblical stance on homosexuality and coming out of its bondage is truly God's stance? And what if true freedom from homosexuality is available for the true seeker? Doesn't that at least make you curious as to how the real truth of the Bible sets you free from homosexuality?

Jesus, right before He went to the cross, prayed to the Father for all His disciples, "'Sanctify them by Your truth. Your word is truth'" (John 17:17). Jesus is praying for His disciples to be set apart unto God by the truth of the Bible. As you have seen throughout this book, God's Word has played a huge role in my change-process so that I was set free from homosexuality and became completely heterosexual in identity, thoughts and feelings, just as I was created to be. And the Word of God continues to be the catalyst that makes me more and more like Christ. Oh, how I praise God for His love and His Scriptures!

If you are new to all of this, you may be thinking, how does reading and knowing all truth in my Bible set me free? As a born again believer, the Spirit of God brings to our minds the precepts and doctrines of truth and applies them with power. These words are heard in the ear, and when they are received in our hearts, they work in us to will and to do God's good pleasure. The truth is the sanctifier, so if we do not hear or read the truth, we will not grow in sanctification and therefore, we will not change. Thus, you must cling to the truth, or these destructive myths will bear much "rotten" fruit. The homosexual will stay stuck in the lifestyle, and the Christian hoping to disciple a new believer will be of very little help.

It is worth repeating over and over, freedom from homosexuality is available to the seeker and it comes in a person, Jesus Christ, who is "'the way, the truth and the life'" (John 14:6). That is why Jesus said, "'Believe in God; believe also in Me" (John 14:1). "'Nor is there salvation in any other, for there is no other name under heaven given to men by which we must be saved'" (Acts 4:12). Oh, dear struggler and seeker, surrender your life to Jesus. His love flowed down from the cross of Calvary for you, just as it did for me. But you must receive His personal love for you with a heart attitude of repentance, and allow Him to be the Lord of your life (Go back and think on chapter 2!). If the Spirit of God is working in your heart now, won't you bow the knee to Lord Jesus today? Please remember, for as long as God has made promises, there have been those who mock His promises, but it is hard to mock a truly changed life! There is hope for the homosexual.

As we have journeyed through the pages of this book, you have found the testimony of all the marvelous works God has done in my life; it is a testimony to the personal love of Jesus that changed my life. Through the words of this book I have spoken the things I have seen and heard in God's Word (Acts 4: 20). By the grace of God working in me, I am what I am (1 Corinthians 15:10). My part throughout the process has been to <u>trust</u> and to <u>obey</u>. What God has accomplished in my life, and in the life of thousands of other ex-homosexuals, He can accomplish in anyone's life.

Well, we have come to that place where our journey together must end. Remember, in the introduction for this book, I shared that God gave me His heart and His vision for all aspects of Bridge of Hope Ministry, which includes the website (www.bridgeofhopeministry.com). Won't you check it out? May this ministry be helpful and truly make a difference in the lives of many people for eternity. May God be glorified as He accomplishes His will in it all! Through all facets of the ministry, I pray many will find real peace and hope for their lives, just as I have. I can truly say, "My hope comes from Him" (Psalm 62:5). As I say goodbye, please believe me when I say it has been a privilege to spend time with you. And this is my closing prayer for you! "Now, may the God of all hope fill you with all joy and peace in believing" (Romans 15:13). Amen!

Notes

Chapter 1

1. Stephen Bennett, "Do You Have a Testimony." *Let Me Show You Jesus*. Sound Source Records, 2001.
2. Alexander Means, "What Wondrous Love." Music by William Walker, 1835.
3. Bill Bright, *Have You Heard of the Four Spiritual Laws?* (Peachtree City, GA: Campus Crusade for Christ, 2000), p. 9.
4. Ibid., p. 10.
5. Bennett, "Do You Have a Testimony."

Chapter 2

1. Bob Davies and Lori Rentzel, *Coming Out of Homosexuality: New Freedom for Men and Women* (Downers Grove, IL: InterVarsity Press, 1993), pp. 20-21.

Chapter 3

1. Ney Bailey, *Faith Is Not a Feeling* (Colorado Springs, CO: WaterBrook Press, 2002), p. 32.

Chapter 4

1. Teresa Muller, "Love Flowed Down." *Love Flowed Down.* Pneuma Music, 2007.

Chapter 5

1. Anne Paulk, *Restoring Sexual Identity: Hope for Women Who Struggle with Same-Sex Attraction* (Eugene, OR: Harvest House Publishers, 2004), p. 30, 46-47.
2. Dee Brestin, *The Friendships of Women* (Colorado Springs, CO: NexGen of Cook Communications Ministries, 2004), pp. 47-63.
3. Davies and Rentzel, *Coming Out of Homosexuality*, p. 38.

Chapter 6

1. Lori Rentzel, *Emotional Dependency* (Downers Grove, IL: InterVarsity Press, 1990), p. 8-9.
2. Dee Brestin, *The Friendships of Women.*
3. Ibid.

Chapter 7

1. Davies and Rentzel, *Coming Out of Homosexuality*, pp. 116-117.
2. Ibid., p. 117.

Chapter 8

1. Oswald Chambers, *My Utmost For His Highest* (Westwood, NJ: Barbour & Co., Inc., 1963), p.170.

Chapter 9

1. Brian McClaren, "On the Homosexual Question: Finding a Pastoral Response."[Weblog entry]. blog. Christianitytoday.com, January 23, 2006.
2. Ibid.
3. Anita Worthen and Bob Davies, *Someone I Love Is Gay: How Family & Friends Can Respond* (Downers Grove, IL: InterVarsity Press, 1996), pp. 147-148.

Chapter 10

1. Timothy J. Dailey, Ph. D., *The Negative Health Effects of Homosexuality.* [Online] 04 May 2006. http://www.frc.org/get.cfm?i=Is01B1
2. David Kupelian, The Marketing of Evil (Nashville, TN: Cumberland House

Publishing, 2005), adapted from chapter 1: Selling Gay Rights to America, pp. 17-38.

3. Pastor Jim Nicodem, *The 7 Myths About Homosexuality*, Christ Community Church: St. Charles, IL, March 30, 2003. CD available at https://www.sbministries.org/appieshop/index.cgi

Printed in the United States
99602LV00001B/169-501/A